CONSTRUCTIVE
ASPECTS OF
ANXIETY

CONSTRUCTIVE
ASPECTS OF
ANXIETY

Edited by
SEWARD HILTNER
and
KARL MENNINGER

Abingdon Press

new york   nashville

CONSTRUCTIVE ASPECTS OF ANXIETY

Copyright © 1963 by Abingdon Press

Library of Congress Catalog Card Number: 63-17825

To

Edward Gallahue

whose conviction it is that the
resources of religion and of
psychiatry can be properly and
intelligently combined to promote
human fulfillment and the purposes
of God

Foreword

In 1954 a unique two-day conference was held at the Menninger Foundation. A dozen clergymen of various denominations and a dozen psychiatrists with various convictions regarding religion assembled in a closed session for frank and friendly interdisciplinary discussion about mutual concerns.

This meeting was made possible by Mr. and Mrs. Edward Gallahue of Indianapolis. Mr. Gallahue has been for many years president of the American States Insurance Company and, also, for many years a member of the Board of Governors of the Menninger Foundation. He himself attended the first conference and most of those that followed, and was so gratified by the obvious satisfaction of the participants that he financed the publication of minutes and papers from the first conference for private circulation. Conferences were held in 1955, 1956, 1957, 1959, and 1960 with the support of Mr. and Mrs. Gallahue.

It was agreed at the very beginning that no one would be quoted by name outside the meeting, but that a committee should be appointed to formulate a statement for public release at the end of the conference. At the first five conferences an evening symposium was thrown open to the psychiatric community, and at the sixth conference (1960) there were two such open meetings. It is the presentations of this 1960 Gallahue Conference which appear in this book, supplemented by Dr. Paul Pruyser's chapter, written at the request of the editors, and by Dr. Seward Hiltner's Epilogue. The second and third chapters, by Dr. Hiltner, are an expansion of the preparatory paper that he wrote in advance of the 1960 conference.

These contributions should be regarded as "work papers"

7

rather than as finished essays. In no sense do they attempt to report the full dialogue between psychiatry and theology even on this one topic. But they sparked much continuing dialogue at the Foundation, and we hope their appearance in print may do the same for others elsewhere.

Anxiety, like pain, is familiar to everyone and fully understood by no one. Whether or not it occurs in animals depends on how it is defined; most of us would say it does indeed. Certainly it is observable in very young human beings. To differentiate anxiety clearly from anxiousness, from apprehensiveness, from concern, from tension, and from various other states of mind or feelings with different appellations is a difficult task indeed. I shall not presume upon the offerings of the contributors, but say only what is well known, namely, that we physicians seem to be of two minds regarding both anxiety and its sister, pain. On the one hand, we see them as part of the world's misery which it is our duty and privilege to attempt to alleviate. On the other hand, we see them as the most reliable instigators of self-help and hence great blessings. They bring the patient to examination and then drive him on through treatment. But in *his* mind pain and anxiety are relentless foes against which the help of therapy is sought.

Theologians, too, may be in a quandary about anxiety. On the one hand they reassure their people with, "Though I walk through the valley of the shadow of death, I shall fear no evil," and with, "Consider the lilies of the field . . . ; they toil not, neither do they spin," and "Perfect love casteth out fear." But, on the other hand, they cry with Job,

> For the thing that I fear comes upon me,
> and what I dread befalls me (R.S.V.),

and with the Psalmist,

> Thy wrath has swept over me;
> thy dread assaults destroy me (R.S.V.),

and they echo such familiar lines as, "Work out your own salvation with fear and trembling."

What could be more suited for a symposium than a topic with such mysterious meanings and implications and contradictions? And who is better fitted for its discussion than a group of men with such varied backgrounds and specialties united by a common bond of concern?

—KARL MENNINGER

Contents

1. Freud's Understanding of Anxiety 15
   Ishak Ramzy

2. Some Theories of Anxiety: Psychiatric 33
   Seward Hiltner

3. Some Theories of Anxiety: Theological 53
   Seward Hiltner

4. Anxious Longing 69
   Fred Berthold, Jr.

5. Anxiety and Grace: An Augustinian Perspective 89
   Albert C. Outler

6. Positive Anxiety in Judaeo-Christian Thought 105
   Charles A. Curran

7. Anxiety: Affect or Cognitive State? 121
   Paul W. Pruyser

   Epilogue 143
   Seward Hiltner

   Contributors Biographical Notes 163

   Index 165

"The ego is the actual seat of anxiety."

Symptoms are created to avoid the outer or inner danger situation of which anxiety sounds the alarm.

—SIGMUND FREUD

CHAPTER I

Freud's Understanding of Anxiety

Ishak Ramzy

Nature! We are surrounded and embraced by her; unable to get away from her, and incapable of going any deeper into her. . . .

For ever and ever she creates new forms. What is now has never been before; what was before never comes again. Everything is new, and nevertheless always old. . . .

Life is her most beautiful invention, and death is her trick to have more life. She envelops man in a haze, and she always prods him toward the light. She stirs needs because she loves movement. . . .

Every need is beneficient, quickly satisfied, quickly again awakened. If she gives another one, this will be a new source of pleasure, but soon she re-establishes the balance. . . .

Her crown is love; only through love can one approach her. She divides all human beings, and they all want to devour each other. She has isolated everything to reunite everything. With a few sips from the chalice of love she rewards for a life of drudgery. . . .

She has set me where I am, and she will lead me forth. To her I trust myself.[1]

These are a few lines from the famous "Essay on Nature," which was attributed to Goethe. Hearing it, around the close of his secondary education, so the story goes, decided the career of the boy who was endowed with a burning, divine curiosity to understand the world within him and around him. The boy lived to become not a natural scientist, like Charles Darwin, nor to study the physical laws of the universe, like Albert Einstein, but to share with these two the credit for changing the course of human knowledge, if not the destiny and the very survival of mankind from the twentieth century onward.

The precocious Sigmund Freud had already been fascinated by the teachings and theories of "The Philosophy of Nature," so that Goethe's essay was just a crystallizing factor that decided his vocation. Thus, the medical school for him was not so much a road that would lead to the practice of medicine, but the best place to equip himself for unraveling the secrets that puzzled him.

Sigmund Freud did not deal with the riddles of the whole universe. He confined himself to the study of man. By the testimony of even those who knew but did not follow his way, he was said to have quite unquestionably done more for the advancement of our understanding of human nature than any other man since Aristotle.

It is important, however, to emphasize that what Freud achieved was not through art, metaphysics, or mystic experience; his studies ranged from physics, physiology, and sociology to logic and philosophy. As if aware of his speculative tendencies, he firmly and consistently schooled himself in the methods of exact science. He familiarized himself with the laws and intricacies of formal logic. Also he came to know and follow the rules and dicta of modern logic, to which he strictly adhered for years in the laboratory as a histologist and later as a psychoanalyst. His assertions were thus founded on the diligent, patient, empirical collection of data, the attempt to put forth a hypothesis, which was to be tested again and again and, if verified, was offered as a theory, still open for correction and addition and at times even not immune from being discarded altogether if the facts did not maintain it.[2]

The teacher who influenced Freud more than any other man in his life was Brücke, who had pledged a solemn oath to prove that no forces other than the physical, chemical ones are active within the organism. Physiology for Brücke was the science of organisms as such, which are only material entities, phenomena of the physical world—systems of atoms, moved by forces according to the principle of conservation of energy. Such a conviction Freud obviously shared with his master.

With this mental set, Freud approached the study of man. And thus, of course, one would not have expected him to be among those who have not seen and yet have believed. On the contrary, his legacy to human knowledge is due mainly to the fact that, in his attempt to establish a science of man, he practiced the motto that a kinsman of his before him had adopted when he said, "Except I shall see in his hands the print of the nails, and put my finger into the print of the nails, and thrust my hand into his side, I will not believe" (John 20:25). Freud chose to doubt until there was no way but to believe.

Freud's Early Understanding of Anxiety

Freud's work on anxiety is an example of this approach. Being such a striking feature of human life, anxiety was one of the earlier concerns for which he suggested an explanation, which he tenaciously held onto. He kept working on it, however, until he was able finally to offer his basic view about it only when he was in the prime age of three score and ten.

Before discussing Freud's views on anxiety, it is perhaps essential to define the term itself. An exact definition, however, cannot be reached unless one has fully understood the essentials and the attributes of a phenomenon. It may suffice, though, to mention that, on the whole, anxiety is a blanket term that covers a wide range of various intensities and colors of unpleasant feelings and affects. It can go from apprehension and timidity to dread, anguish, panic, and terror; or it can be just a trace of abashment, clumsiness, embarrassment, or confusion. Common to all the intensities of this type of unpleasant feeling is a vague sense of something impending, a dreaded expectation of something harmful or painful. We have come to mean still further by anxiety a wide array and a curious admixture of feelings that may cover also the area of remorse, contrition, guilt, and depression—to mention only a few.

The simplest and the most accurate way of defining anxiety, however, is perhaps to contrast it with its opposite, which is peace—peace of the mind. On the eastern shores of the Mediterranean, where ancient tongues are still spoken, when people meet or separate from each other, they do not say "good morning" or "good-bye"; they wish each other peace, whatever the time of the day and however the situation may be.

The search for a way out of anxiety is evidently as old as man's awareness of himself. But Freud was neither a historian nor an anthropologist. He wanted to understand, through being a physician, the individual, the particular, the concrete. He was confronted, as were his colleagues, with the problem of anxiety when he started to practice neuropsychiatry. Although there was already some inkling that some kind of therapy, called at the time "mental treatment," might be the effective way of helping those who suffered from unbearable anxiety, it was said that "though you speak to them with the tongues of angels and possess the eloquence of the prophets, you will not succeed in detaching them from their tormenting situation." [3] The failure, of course, was due to the prevalence of theories that only gave lip service to mental phenomena and in all seriousness suggested explanations connected with certain parts of the nervous system, where anxiety resided or bravery generated.

In the early years of his practice Freud used to help his patients by whatever means he had been taught or thought acceptable; but in his attempt to unravel the reasons for their suffering, he blocked everything except his wish to understand human beings as a physiologist, who ultimately might explain them not only in terms of physics but even in terms of mathematics. Freud until the early nineties of the last century still was under the illusion of his time; namely, that of explaining mental life in terms of the anatomy and physiology of the brain. So he started to write a "Psychology for Neurologists," later known as the "Project for a Scientific Psychology." [4] This ambitious piece of work, published only posthumously, was mainly an attempt to reduce mental phenomena to cerebral physiology; and contrary to his plan, this was where Freud inadvertently let the philosopher in him run astray. That so-called scientific project turned out to be just a deductive, speculative venture, feverishly performed in a hurry, as if the impact of nonorganic data were threatening Freud's faith in biology and neurology, so he had to save it before it was superseded by psychology proper.

It is interesting to note that in this book he never mentioned the word "anxiety"; he talked only in terms of pain and unpleasure. Anxiety was to be witnessed in patients, talked about in other papers, but not in scientific psychology. Pleasure and unpleasure for Freud, the stubborn scientist, were only to be considered in terms of quantities of excitation and the capacity to handle excessive stimulation. He implicitly considered anxiety as unpleasure that is related to earlier pain experiences; so that "if the memory-image of the hostile [that is, pain-giving] object is in any manner freshly cathected, a condition arises which is not pain, but has a similarity to pain." Pain itself was explained with the help of the concept of the protective barrier; that is, the screen that has the function of shielding the organism from the floods of stimuli which impinge on it. Whenever this protective barrier is pierced, pain is generated. This concept of pain as a "breach of continuity" is as ancient in medicine as Galen, and was conveyed to Western Europe by Avicenna, Galen's messenger to Europe until the eighteenth century. It is interesting to note that Avicenna considered pain as a result of something contrary to the course of nature, and reiterated that "all this can be reduced to the one essential thing—loss of continuity and nothing more." [5] It is also striking that we shall later come across this very same concept in the understanding of anxiety, but in another context and from another level.

That early attempt of Freud demonstrates his intention to find out the physiological basis for mental phenomena, normal and pathological, or, to put it simply, to resolve the perennial problem of body and mind. Although by the passage of time this hope lost its hold on him, still it lurked in his thinking till his latter years. It perhaps lurks still in the minds of all analysts: the hope that neurophysiology will one day provide the answer.

Freud's first direct and more sober attempt to understand anxiety was, of course, still colored by that approach. His major paper of this period dealing with the subject was written in 1894 under the title of "The Justification for Detaching from Neurasthenia a Particular Syndrome: The Anxiety-Neurosis." [6] After a short introduction, Freud handled the topic in an orderly manner. First he described the clinical symptomatology of anxiety-neurosis and gave an exhaustive account of its manifestations: general irritability, anxious expectation, common nervousness, hypochondria. It is worth noting that he included and underlined "pangs of conscience" in this category—all of which in his words are characterized by "a quantum of anxiety in a free-floating condition." There are also the sudden eruptions of anxiety attacks without any associated idea, as well as those associated with an idea such as that of sudden death, of a stroke, or of insanity. He went on to enumerate the physical concomitants and equivalents of anxiety, such as the disturbances of heart functions and respiration, attacks of perspiration and tremors, ravenous hunger, diarrhea, vertigo, vasomotor attacks, and paresthesia. To this he added the description of night terrors and two groups of phobias; one connected with common physiological dangers, such as the fear of snakes, thunderstorms, bugs, and the like, and the second including fears limiting movement, such as agoraphobia. Freud concluded the list by an account of the gastrointestinal disturbances and the sensory and muscular ailments in anxiety-neurosis.

In the next section Freud dealt with the incidence and etiology of anxiety, and here he stated that it was advisable to treat men and women separately. In the female he mentioned what he called virginal anxiety or anxiety in adolescents, anxiety in the newly married, anxiety in women whose husbands suffer from impaired potency or practice coitus interruptus or reservatus, anxiety in widows and the voluntarily abstinent, and anxiety in the climacteric. In men he also set up groups similar to those among women and added that anxiety-neurosis can arise in both sexes from factors which are not of a sexual nature at all, such as overwork, sick-nursing, or severe illness.

In the last section of this paper Freud presented a theory of the anxiety-neurosis built mainly on two arguments: The first is that "we are dealing here with an accumulation of excitation," and the second is "the exceedingly important fact that the anxiety, which underlies all the clinical symptoms of the neurosis, is not derived from any psychical source," but is due to the automatic transformation of the dammed-up erotic urge into anxiety.

Any objections raised later against this somatic, toxicological theory of anxiety were firmly brushed aside by Freud. When Löwenfeld dared to criticize it, Freud lectured him on the principles of etiology in medicine. For years Jones tried politely to refute it as untenable on both the biological and psychological grounds, but Freud seemed only to lend him a deaf ear. And when Stekel pointed out that he had frequently met with the same conflicts and complexes in all patients, neurasthenic or neurotic, Freud shrugged it off, saying that Stekel greatly exaggerated psychogenesis.

For many years Freud set aside any other explanation of anxiety, but it seems that he himself had an inkling that he had trespassed with this view far beyond the actual observations. He continued collecting more data from his clinical practice, and from time to time added some remarks in connection with the manifestations or the equivalents of anxiety that he observed in the various forms of neurotic illness. But his primary stand long remained unchanged.

In the meantime, he was able to achieve that which made his contributions such an epoch-making step in the history of human thought. This can be concisely summarized in the two or three following points.

First, Freud undertook the most risky project of his life, which was to undergo psychoanalysis. The risk involved in this matter can hardly be appreciated in our time; but when it is realized that Freud had no company, no help, no precedent, it can be imagined what a degree of moral and intellectual courage he must have mustered. From his unique venture into the bewildering expanses of man's inner self, Freud did not emerge confused or tongue-tied, but was able, in his magnum opus, *The Interpretation of Dreams*,[7] to tell the story of what he had seen.

His findings were not to remain long in the realm of theory or leisurely exploration; they were soon adopted into his practice. Having tried to help his patients with electrotherapy and having prescribed drugs, baths, and massage, and then having used suggestion and hypnosis—all of which satisfied neither his rational attitude nor his therapeutic goals—he hit upon a new method of investigation and of therapy, which came to be known as psychoanalysis. This, in a way, can be described as the application of scientific method to the understanding of man as a whole, not in bits and pieces.

His work, both on himself and on others, led Freud to the most momentous discovery that he ever made. It is not accurate that what perturbed the world were his views on infantile sexuality or his emphasis on the nonmorality of man or his destructive urges or death wishes. It was that Freud dealt the heaviest blow ever aimed at man's vanity by his discovery of the unconscious. It is this, probably more than anything else, that made the world resent Freud. True, many a thinker before him had hinted or talked about the unconscious, but never in a way to prove that it was really there. By demonstrating that the larger and more important portion of the person's mental life happens without his awareness, Freud told man that he is not master over even himself.

Freud's Later Understanding of Anxiety

Thus passed about three decades after Freud announced his first opinion on anxiety, during which he was busy establishing a comprehensive working hypothesis of human psychology. When Freud came to pick up the problem of anxiety again, he dealt with it in a whole book, which is one of the most important and intricate classics of the discipline, and offered a view different from the first one.

Even his style and his manner of presentation were different. Contrary to his habit, there was neither a prelude nor a statement of the problem that might prepare the reader for the main theme of the book. It was as if he were planning to make a completely fresh start or to turn a new leaf, so as to arrive directly at the conclusion of his life's work.

Inhibitions, Symptoms and Anxiety[8] differentiates between inhibition, which is mainly a reduction of function, not necessarily pathological, and symptom, which is a morbid process and an alteration of function.[6] A symptom is a result of the attempt to find a substitute for the lack of gratification, a process which starts once the person perceives a signal of danger. The most important statement in this sequence is where Freud says: "The ego is the actual seat of anxiety." This concept was radically different from his previous views: Whereas anxiety had been supposed to generate somewhere in the body—in the seminal vesicles, the subcortical regions, or in whatever location the toxic transformation happened—anxiety was now considered to be in man's mind.

Freud then, in more than one chapter, describes the development of the various functions of the ego, which include, not only perception and control of action and organization of thinking, but also the various devices to block or allay the anxiety that would generate if man's animal heritage were let loose, with the unavoidable clash bound to ensue between the various aspects of the personality or between the individual and those around him. Freud corroborates this view with clinical examples and revises some of his earlier intervening views about mental functioning, then concludes this part by stating that symptoms are created to avoid the outer or inner danger situation of which anxiety sounds the alarm. He proceeds to draw a series of important equations involving danger situations, such as the infantile experience of separation from the mother's breast, the baby's reactions to the loss of its body contents, and the boy's anxiety over his genitals, up to the fear of death itself. Once he has done this, he redefines anxiety as the reaction to, or the threat of, a loss or a separation.

With this we reach the central theme of the book. Addressing himself to the nature of anxiety, Freud was able to give the following answer: An anxiety state is a reproduction of an early experience that becomes perceived and felt as something unpleasant, accompanied by various physical sensations and physiological changes.

As to what it is a recollection of, nothing is more obvious than birth itself. Even the roots of the word "anxiety," in more than one family of languages, are related to narrow passages or to being besieged. But here Freud disowns his earlier complete acceptance of the traumatic effects of birth, because whatever the distress or the danger in birth, it is nothing more than a gross physiological disturbance, which cannot have any psychic content. The newborn, Freud emphasizes, cannot conceivably be aware of going through an experience before he has enough mental equipment with which to perceive it, an equipment that has to take some time before it becomes an actuality, not just a potential constitutional capacity. It is only when the mental functions have developed enough that the baby starts to be afraid; that is, of being left alone or left in the dark or left with a strange person. Such instances can be reduced to a single condition; namely, "that of missing someone who is loved and longed-for"—and who else more than the mother or the mothering person?

But why is there that much distress over the separation from the mother? Why that much longing, which never leaves man all through his life but is with him always in one form or another? No one would disagree with Freud's concise statement:

> The reason why the infant in arms wants to perceive the presence of its mother is only because it already knows by experience that she gratifies all its needs without delay. The situation, then, that it regards as a "danger" and against which it wants to be safeguarded is one of nongratification, of a growing tension due to need, against which it is helpless. I think that if we adopt this view, all the facts fall into place.[9]

To put it simply, Freud considered that anxiety is a signal which reminds the person of his helplessness without love and protection.

The psychoanalytic viewpoint about anxiety thus carries the following implications:

First, man is bound to be always anxious. His anxiety is due to the threat of his animal nature which, if let loose, can seldom, if ever, except in infancy, be fully gratified. So generate feelings of helplessness, rage, and loneliness. What makes things harder still is that, at the same time, man acquires through his imagination and the ideals fostered by civilization a fantastic picture of self-control and perfection. Thus he is also mortified whenever he unavoidably comes short of that image of perfection, which is far beyond his limited powers and contradicts his animal urges. Harder still, and paradoxically enough, his animal nature and his godly ambitions can very often get together against him, which only adds to his despair and agony.

Second, man has even lost the capacity to be afraid. It is puzzling why Freud rarely used the word "fear" and more often than not preferred to use the term *real Angst,* or "objective anxiety." This is probably because Freud considered that only man can be anxious. Fear is an attribute of the animal, which can react to danger almost like an automaton and in response to a definite stimulus, or of a god—if fear can be an attribute of a god, who by definition has the omniscience that makes him know exactly where to draw the line between what is real and objective and what is personal and subjective.

Third, once anxiety is recognized as a universal, unavoidable condition of human existence and the factors that contribute to its genesis and exacerbation are empirically studied, our ability to alleviate it is increased.

This brings us to the fourth point, which is therapy. The core of psychoanalytic therapy is the attempt to reinstate a situation similar to that within which anxiety used to arise and then with the help of reason to try to find new solutions better than the old. The analyst, who is often maligned and at times deified, is just a person who tries to avoid being told, "And why beholdest thou the mote that is in thy brother's eye, but perceivest not the beam that is in thine own eye" (Luke 6:41). Before attempting to help others out of their anxiety, the analyst must have sought help about it himself, and all through his work he does know that the distance between the couch and the chair is too small to allow himself pride or vanity.

Anxiety and Creativity

In connection with creativity, if the emphasis is on the signal function of anxiety, it will be readily recognized that anxiety is of no positive use as such. An alarm clock can be set to wake a person at a certain time, but the rings of its bell, loud or soft, would not tell him what to do or where to go when he gets up. One person can start his day by saying the morning prayers or by getting ready to perform a surgery, water the spring flowers, or write a poem; another person may get up to set off a bomb that might destroy a well-established place of worship or bring down to its roots a place of learning and recreation.

And if the emphasis is put on anxiety, whatever its nature or source may be, one can very simply say that it may lead to some creativeness, but very little if any at all of the credit would go to anxiety as such. Instead of the widely held, erroneous conviction that anxiety is a prerequisite for creativity, it can be maintained that anxiety often blocks the creative process, or at times may instead drive it mercilessly and blindly. The result in the latter instance is that creations will be of a much lesser quality than the talent of him who has created, and the expression will be restricted to repetitive themes and forms, or to monotonous rebellions. Ample evidence for this assertion could be drawn from such fields as art, literature, science, and music or even from ordinary life and clinical observations.

To put it in another way, the very presence of anxiety continually drains man's energy and detracts from his capacity for enjoyment and his ability to bring about newer forms of comfort, expression, and growth. In his attempt to get away from the throes of anxiety, a man may become a painter, a scientist, a writer, together with or without one or the other syndrome. In either case, some gift is needed, among other things, to resort to the creative attempt besides the pathological one. The creativity out of anxiety will essentially remain the production of the driven and the slave. The individual in such an instance may derive some solace from what he creates, may or may not eventually reap some reward for his creativity, but it will not ultimately provide him an escape from his unresolved conflict or his inner turmoil.

It is tempting to speculate here about the motives for the emergence and the perpetuation of that erroneous belief. Could it not be that people, who naturally differ in their inborn abilities, become envious of him who is able to create in spite of suffering? Could it be that this is why they wish to foster the idea that anxiety is necessary for him? Could it not be that by this they aim to achieve two purposes: first, to tell themselves, "Well, what does it profit a man to gain a whole world of fantasy and lose himself?" and second, to keep on exploiting the poor fellow instead of attempting to give him a hand or to share with him some of what they have? And the poor fellow would be only too ready to believe them, also, for two possible reasons: The first is due to the hold of anxiety on him, which, like a demon, would not let him go in peace. And the second, which may be derived at least partly from this, is his suspicion that he may, after all, have much less talent than he wants himself and others to believe he has.

Those who are familiar with the literature of psychoanalysis may be inclined to comment that the whole theory of sublimation in psychoanalytic psychology is still obscure and incomplete. In this they are right, but what about the matter from another point of view? What about the ethical goals we like to think the whole civilization of mankind in such a comparatively short time has been trying steadily, though gropingly and haltingly, to achieve? Does not the belief that anxiety is essential for production sound like the argument that underfed cotton-pickers in the fields and workers in sweat shops were essential to preserve the structure or maintain the progress of society?

Anxiety, Reason, and Religion

It is no secret that Freud discussed methods other than psycho-analysis that man employs to cope with his anxiety. One of these was religion, and Freud's opinion was firm and decisive. He considered religion as derived from the anxieties connected with the little boy's situation between his mother and father, and explained away the formalities and rituals of worship as the obsessional neurosis of mankind. Some of his pupils have gone further and have held the view that man's great need for God is a means to overcome deep human despair. Faith is said to achieve its therapeutic success through the same means by which the earliest depressions of our infancy are handled; namely, by restitution for the damage that we believe was done to the parents, especially the mother. The idea of an intact, merciful, and beneficent figure is a gleam of light to dispel some of the darkness of man's infantile guilt.

It is obvious that such an explanation is derived from the genetic approach, which is not the only way in the search for truth. On the other hand, it is no more sufficient to dismiss Freud's views on religion as a genetic fallacy than it is for him and his pupils to dismiss the contributions of religion to man's moral development and his cultural achievements. Further still, we live now at a time when physicists and astrobiologists are discussing such topics as infinity, immortality, antimatter, and the probability of higher forms of life in the universe. A huge radio telescope has been built, partly to listen to messages which scientists say, because of our ignorance and stupidity, we have not heard before. At such a time, some analysts may admit that the existence of entities other than man and more powerful and advanced than he, would better be left to those who are proficient in other disciplines of knowledge.

One thing, however, the pupils of Freud seem to remain certain of: It is only when, or inasmuch as, the soft but persistent voice of reason has rescued man's freedom and intelligence from the shackles of his neurosis that he may be liberated enough to join that pious woman of old who, amidst the firm tradition of

Moses, Jesus, and Mohammed, was able to raise her voice and say, "I love the Lord for what He is, not out of any fear of His punishment nor in expectation of any reward."

References

1. Johann Wolfgang von Goethe, "Die Natur," *Goethes Werke,* 1900, XXX, 413-18.
2. Ishak Ramzy, "From Aristotle to Freud," *Bulletin of the Menninger Clinic,* 1956, XX, 413-418.
3. Ernest Jones, *Papers on Psycho-Analysis* (4th ed.; London: Bailliere, Tindall & Cox, 1938).
4. Sigmund Freud, "Project for a Scientific Psychology," *The Origins of Psycho-Analysis,* ed. Marie Bonaparte et al, trans. Eric Mosbacher and James Strachey (New York: Basic Books Inc., Publishers, 1954).
5. Oskar Cameron Gruner, *Treatise on the Canon of Medicine of Avicenna* (London: Luzac, 1930).
6. Freud (1894), "The Justification for Detaching from Neurasthenia a Particular Syndrome: The Anxiety-Neurosis," *Collected Papers,* 1924, I, 76-106.
7. Freud, "The Interpretation of Dreams," *Standard Edition of the Complete Psychological Works of Sigmund Freud,* general ed. and trans. James Strachey (24 vols.; New York: The Macmillan Co., 1953). Used by permission of The Hogarth Press and Basic Books, Inc. Vols. IV-V.
8. Freud, *Inhibitions, Symptoms and Anxiety,* trans. Alix Strachey (London: The Hogarth Press, 1936).
9. *Ibid.*

"Where we are dealing with anxiety, everything is in a state of flux and change."

"The difficulty does not lie in the incompleteness of our observations. . . . No, it is genuinely a question of hypotheses . . . , of the introduction of the right abstract ideas."

—SIGMUND FREUD

CHAPTER II

Some Theories of Anxiety: Psychiatric

Seward Hiltner

In the previous chapter, Ishak Ramzy has shown the development that took place in Freud's understanding of anxiety from earlier to later phases of his work and thought. The present chapter will concentrate on Freud's later theory of anxiety. Brief attention will be given to the thought of other psychiatrists and psychologists about anxiety. But the focus will be on trying to grasp the very far-reaching implications of Freud's latest theory.

In the following chapter two theological theories of anxiety will be presented, one by Sören Kierkegaard and Reinhold Niebuhr, and the other by Paul Tillich.

The present chapter and the chapter following have been retained in the descriptive form in which they were first written, where together they served as an advance paper for the Gallahue Conference. I have subsequently expanded the material and, for purposes of convenience, divided it into two chapters. Since Ramzy's discussion of Freud deals with the whole range of Freud's thought about anxiety, whereas my discussion of Freud focuses on the later theory, it has seemed best for the present chapter to follow Ramzy's discussion.

The most comprehensive account of modern theories of anxiety and of discoveries about anxiety from the several sciences was given by Rollo May in 1950.[1] For summaries of findings and points of view in the biological, psychological, and social sciences about anxiety, we refer the reader especially to that work.

We call the reader's attention also to another important study of anxiety for which one of the contributors to this volume, Ishak Ramzy, is principally responsible, but which cannot, for reasons of space, be presented in our book.[2] This study attempts to consider the interrelationship between pain and anxiety and begins with Freud's theory of pain as well as with his theory of anxiety. The authors hypothesize that there are several kinds of connections between physical and mental pain, and especially that a person's capacity to tolerate both probably derives from the same kinds of sources. The authors regard the principal merit of their hypothesis as methodological, since the possible correlation of pain and anxiety may make it possible to use study devices that have not ordinarily been considered relevant to anxiety.

We turn now directly to an elaboration of Freud's later theory of anxiety.

Freud's Later Theory

Almost from the beginning of his work, as the account by Ramzy in the first chapter makes clear, Freud recognized anxiety to be a basic theoretical as well as clinical problem. As psychoanalysis expanded and developed in the light of its growing clinical penetration, the theoretical problem of anxiety became more important. The greater the clinical wisdom about anxiety, the more difficult and yet necessary was a fundamental theoretical understanding of it. The more complexities were taken into account, the greater was the danger of doing them less than justice in the general theory.

In one of his last discussions of anxiety, Freud expressed the conviction that the theory of anxiety was "in a state of flux and change."[3] He did not imply, in that discussion, that better or deeper or clearer theory would emerge automatically as clinical wisdom advanced. Useful as relevant data always are, what is needed, Freud wrote, is better intellectual synthesis. "It is genuinely a question of hypotheses . . . , of the introduction of the right abstract ideas, and of their application to the raw material of observation so as to bring order and lucidity into it."[4]

The most important thing said by Freud in his mature theory

of anxiety was about its function. When danger is sensed and a signal given so the organism may act or react in relation to the danger, the function of anxiety is being performed.[5] Anxiety is, so to speak, an alarm clock. It warns of some danger. If it is possible for the person to hear the alarm and then to mobilize his resources, he can do "something to avoid the situation or retreat from it." [6] By fight, flight, or adaptation, he is able, after heeding the alarm, to do something relevant in relation to it. If he succeeds in doing so, then the purpose for which the alarm rang has been fulfilled. The alarm is then stilled until needed again. Its warning having been heeded and its function thus performed, it has triggered off (but not empowered) appropriate action concerning whatever danger it rang about. When the process moves this way, the normative function of anxiety has been performed. The alarm has stimulated needed action and it may stop ringing.

It should be noted that in this view of Freud the same basic function is being performed, whatever the nature or source of the danger about which anxiety rings the alarm. The response a man should make to a signal about his mortality ought indeed to be different from one that concerns an unresolved Oedipus complex, but the alarm function is the same in both instances. Or one man's signal may be about failing to use his powers, while another man's may concern his profligate waste of them. The signal is, in both cases, a message rather than a proclamation, in that it carries the equivalent of full name and address.

If the phenomenon known as anxiety always performs its normative function, thus leading to its own dissipation by triggering appropriate response to the particular danger situation, it would always be constructive and would, therefore, not be the concern it is to psychiatry and psychoanalysis. Manifestly this is not the actual situation. Instead what happens very often is this: Symptoms are created in order to avoid the *danger situation* of which anxiety sounds the alarm.[7] There *is* a danger situation. The anxiety signal begins to ring. If the person hears the ring, he will have to acknowledge the danger it is ringing about. This he cannot do because a great deal of his psychic energy has been used to

35

construct an edifice, through dynamics like repression, that prevents him from giving even the barest diplomatic recognition to this actually existing danger. If, despite all the previous psychic prestidigitation, the alarm is now beginning to ring, some new way must quickly be found to prevent the need to look squarely at the danger. This new way, generally speaking, is "symptoms." This is a new order of defense against acknowledging the nature of the danger by first not having to acknowledge the signal about the danger. Thus the capacity to heed the alarm and the development of symptoms tend to be mutually exclusive. It was reflection upon this clinical observation that led Freud to this aspect of his theory.

If the warning signal of anxiety is heard and heeded and if whatever can be done is done in relation to the danger situation, the signal is turned off until next time. By analogy, the person hearing the alarm clock gets out of bed, mobilizes his clothes or his breakfast, and turns off the clock. But instead of hearing the clock, various things may be done to or with it. One person may reach out, eyes closed, and throw a pillow over it. Another, also allegedly asleep, may even toss it out the window. A third may bury his head in a pillow, and a fourth may later argue that he thought it was the telephone ringing. All such devices are analogous to symptoms. They make it apparently unnecessary to meet the situation by first dimming or eliminating the ringing of the alarm.

At the level of the ordinary world of conscious purposes, tasks, and realities, it is plain that the hocus pocus with the alarm clock entails penalties. Breakfast is missed or snatched on the run, the children leave for school before father can bid them good-bye, shaving must be passed up until evening, and an important business deal falters because of tardiness. But these losses do not stand alone. Over against them is the "secondary gain" of not having to experience the pain that would come if one really confronted the danger situation, which is accomplished by the compromise of not even hearing the alarm. Even though the clock analogy should not be pushed too far, it may be that our man who heard it late finds "secondary gain" in punishing himself nutritionally, in not having to face fatherhood, in retreating to roughness via whiskers, or in expressing the wish to fail by not making the business deal. In both a metaphorical and a literal sense, laziness is not sufficient explanation for many oversleepers.

We now reach what is, in many respects, the most crucial point about Freud's last theory of anxiety. When the alarm is not heard and heeded but triggers off symptoms instead of adaptation, *what* is it that has gone wrong? The crucial answer is: Whatever has gone wrong, it is not necessarily the signaling system itself. Whether the alarm clock or father's head is covered by pillows, the clock goes on ringing. Without denying that the clock may be dealt with in terms of such violence that it breaks, in the psychic life this happens but rarely. Whatever is wrong, it is only in minor degree the alarm capacity in itself. Indeed it is the resilience and endurance of the signaling-capacity that may prove to be the basis of some constructive aspects of anxiety.

For our present purposes it is not necessary to discuss in detail what has failed when the anxiety signal, instead of being heard, is followed by symptoms. Freud saw the culprit of this failure as the ego. The ego lacks the power to deal with the danger situation without pain, or it lacks the courage to approach the danger despite some pain, or it has become so habituated to the use of avoidance mechanisms that it automatically puts its motor into the denial gear. When anxiety fails in its pointing intent, what is at fault is not the signaling capacity but rather the incapacity of the person (or ego) to confront the danger being warned about, and hence his incapacity even to accept warning that a danger exists.

Anxiety and Affect in Freud's Theory

In Freud's view, what is the relationship between anxiety and affect? We may look, in the first instance, at this relationship when the signal has been heard, when appropriate adaptive procedures have been taken, and as a result when the alarm has gone back into quiescence. In these situations the important fact is that affect is temporary. Whether it is strong or weak, it is dissipated by the relatively successful adaptive behavior. And however strong it may be, it is not strong enough to paralyze all adaptive action, since some such action has been taken.

Even when the affect is weak or very short-lived, however, it partakes of the quality connoted by a "characteristic tightening in the breathing." [8] Freud rightly noted the derivation of the German *Angst* from the Latin *angustia,* which means "a strait" or "a narrow place." [9] Thus the affect normal to hearing the signal of danger that is anxiety is constrictive but temporary. One thinks analogously of driving a car at high speed on a good highway as like the situation before the alarm has been rung. When suddenly a narrow and dangerous bridge looms ahead, the perception of this is like the signal itself. The sense of narrowing, of constriction, of tightening of the breath that occurs at once, as one tries to guide his car through the narrow place, is not pleasant. But instead of paralyzing him or leading him to crash by too much wheel or too heavy brakes, it has given him an accurate perception of his need to "narrow," to guide the car within a fraction of an inch rather than by a couple of feet as will suffice in most driving. And even though the temporary constricting affect was, after a fashion, painful, the driver was, so to speak, too busy to feel himself feeling it while it was going on. The chances are that he will feel himself feeling it only after he has crossed the bridge. If he is wise, he will roll slowly to a stop after a half mile or so and let his affect calm down a bit before he begins to drive again. After he has stopped, he may indeed verbalize, even repetitively, the experience through which he has just come. This is clearly an attempt to "master the situation." By this time what has happened is felt as a minor trauma. Thus the retrospective handling of it is initially like Freud's "compulsion to repeat." But the *real* danger situation has in fact now passed. One has already mastered it. The verbal or recollective retracing of the ground is to assure oneself that the mastery has actually occurred. Affect may still be high. But one may now look at himself feeling the affect, when the overall situation shows: first, that his having had the affect at the danger point was proper; and second, that the affect did trigger off whatever was needed to get him through the crisis.

Implicitly we have distinguished two levels of affect: first, the feeling at the hearing of the signal and the immediate resulting adaptive action; and second, the perception of the self feeling the affect, retrospectively to the point of danger and contemporaneously at the hangovers of constriction. Since the last is what provides the experience of "psychic pain," it is fair to say that it "hurt" more after crossing the bridge than during the crossing. The subjective experience of psychic pain or hurt involves feeling ourselves feeling the hurt. Even when the signal has been strong, the danger real, and the feeling of constriction during the period of adaptation great, one does not have time to feel himself feeling the constriction. This he can do only in retrospect.

A third level of affect may also be distinguished. After a period of retrospect, our driver can start his car again. And for an hour or a day he may continue the explicit process of feeling himself feeling the constrictive affect by viewing it in retrospect. But something will also be new in his perceptions of the future. When on a beautiful stretch of road, he may go a bit more slowly than before lest he find, around the next curve, a narrow bridge. A slight residuum of the traumatic affect becomes a part of his "alertness." If this is only slightly constricting and helps him to be more alert to unexpected danger, this fact will not injure him, and may some day save his own life and that of others. The affective residue of the traumatic experience is to aid, in the future, the heeding of the danger signal even more quickly and accurately than before. But affect as a continuation of constrictive feeling almost paralyzing in its pressure is *not* involved.

Like all analogies, this one has its deficiencies. Not all danger situations are external. Not all approach us suddenly. Not all can be conquered in a matter of seconds. Not all provide for a cleancut, all-or-nothing conquest of the danger. For the points covered, the analogy seems useful. It should not be stretched beyond them.

We have seen then that when anxiety performs its signaling function and normative results ensue, the affect accompanying the crisis is high but there is little feeling of it as "hurt," while that following the crisis "hurts" but the hurt is tolerable, because there is clear proof that the danger has been passed, and that the long-term effect of the crisis in affect is constructive in regard to capacity for further adaptation.

What, in Freud's view, is the relationship of affect to anxiety when the normative procedure does *not* take place, when, to begin with, the signal of danger is not heard? The general answer is that, whatever specific form the affect may take, "the affective state is paralyzing and unadapted to the present situation." [10] This may sound tautologous unless it is recalled that, according to Freud, affect may be conscious or unconscious and in varying degrees. Various dynamics, of which repression is the prototype, may divorce conscious awareness from processes that are going on in the physical organism and that have counterparts in the organism viewed from a psychic perspective. Thus there is implicit in Freud's account a continuum model of the relationship between anxiety and affect.

We have already examined one extreme of the continuum— what happens when the danger signal is heard and heeded. Coming next on the continuum (and moving toward increasing degrees of pathology) is the conscious feeling of a "free-floating, general apprehensiveness" or "expectant dread." [11] The signal, we might say, has been heard; and, while the stridency of the ring may have been toned down, it has not been covered with pillows or thrown out the window. But for various kinds of reasons, the hearing of the signal has not resulted in correct identification of the danger situation, followed by appropriate adaptation. Further as Freud's "general apprehensiveness" and "expectant dread" suggest, there is a tendency to "futurize" the danger instead of looking for it in the contemporary situation. If the alarm, however toned down, is still ringing, and yet one has not located the danger, then the danger must be on the way, but not yet here. Once a futurizing stance is taken, there is, so to speak, a new defense against examining the true nature of the danger already at hand. It is as if one said, "I've already looked and it isn't here." Clini-

cally speaking, the fact that a free-floating and general apprehensiveness is consciously registered does indicate that the connection between awareness and the present underlying danger
situation has not been cut.

But the related clinical point is no less important; the indefinite
continuation of this kind of affect (or habituation to it as if it
were the normal condition) is itself an indication that the real
danger situation has not been recognized much less dealt with.
It cannot be denied that such a person experiences some kind
of suffering and tends to evoke pity. But a closer inspection shows
him as watching himself feel his feelings, and thus his consciously
experienced affect is less than he believes it to be. To return to
the automobile analogy, he is like the driver who managed to stop
the car before getting onto the bridge, and who now quakingly
watches himself as he was and could be—but who thus avoids the
whole question of getting across the bridge and beyond. He has
constrictive affect and some good reason for it. But the affect is
not entirely what it appears to be, and it defends the person from
the necessity of negotiating the bridge.

On Freud's implied continuum the next place, moving toward
pathology, is occupied by the "phobias." [12] Here too the conscious
awareness of a constrictive affect continues, but it is attached to
specific types of objects or situations in which there is at least
some considerable element of displacement from the real danger
situation. Freud's classic exposition of this was the horse phobia
in the case of Little Hans.[13] Here too the connection between
consciously felt affect and what is going on underneath is not cut.
But whereas the "free-floating, general apprehensiveness" is wait-
ing for a future diagnosis, the "phobia" has abstracted and made a
false diagnosis. When confronted with the object of its apprehensiveness, it can shake and suffer. But the suffering is mitigated
because this is an affliction of fate, and one can pity himself suffering. In addition, he can utilize his adaptive capacities to avoid
encounter with the phobic type of object. Thus this reaction is
one degree further along the continuum toward pathology than
is general conscious apprehensiveness. The cement barriers be-

tween the periods of painful affect and the possibility of having to deal with the real danger situation are much thicker than in "expectant dread."

The third step on Freud's implicit continuum is affect as it occurs in "hysteria and in other severe neuroses." [14] He notes that this may either accompany "symptoms" or manifest itself independently "whether as an attack or as a condition which persists for some time." [15] In the hysterical or convertive forms, there is an even greater separation (than in expectant dread or phobia) between the underlying danger situation and conscious affect. What brings the person with a hysterically paralyzed arm to the physician involves no painful conscious awareness of the danger concealed by this compromise formation and is probably not mainly the pain of the arm. It is the conscious fear of an armless future. Since such a fear is rational and realistic, it relieves consciousness of any trace of affect involving responsibility or guilt or inadequacy. Further, it deals passively with adaptation. Repairing the arm is the doctor's job. If it can not be repaired, then the physician is poor, or medicine inadequate. Here the distance between danger situation and affect is great.

Freud is not explicit as to where on the hypothetical continuum reactions would fall in which there are not only "symptoms" but also occasional "attacks" of affect in the form of acute constriction of feeling. There are two possibilities. On the one hand, the acute attack might lead to making the symptom more rigid and impervious, in which case this reaction would be farther toward the pathological end of the continuum than a symptom like hysterical conversion unaccompanied by an occasional attack. But on the other hand, such an attack might lead to a recognition that the symptom *is* a symptom, and hence lead to a more relevant form of adaptive behavior such as getting psychiatric assistance. Clinically, both things may be observed. The panic attack is probably to be interpreted as a new, and sometimes a "last gasp," attempt by the anxiety alarm to be heard. Whether the hearing leads to new attempts at adaptation that are more appropriate or to throwing more pillows over the clock depends on the relative strength in the person of the factors that led originally to the formation of symptoms, to one kind of symptom rather than another, and to whether anything new has been added (as by therapy) in the interim.

It is not clear in Freud's account what position is occupied by an acute attack in the person who does not have symptoms, except that the attack is a very loud form of warning. Since this shows the strength and durability of the signaling system, it is like the attempt to lead the reluctant and screaming child to the bathtub after all suggestions concerning the virtues of soap and water have proved unavailing. But what this will do in relation to the *next* bath is ambiguous. Symptoms may arise to avoid the possibility of another acute attack, as the child may avoid bathing by illness. Or if the bath is what it should be, the child may lose some of his reluctance and next time take it with less need for extreme measures.

If the affect is a "condition which persists for some time," this might be like the "free-floating, general apprehensiveness," which would move it farther from the pathological end of the continuum. Or it might mean that the general aura of apprehensiveness and quaking has itself become a defense against any genuinely apprehensive feeling, in which case it would belong at about the "symptoms" point.

Although Freud does not explicitly discuss the more psychotic forms of psychopathology in relation to affect and anxiety, it seems clear that the movement toward greater pathology tends generally to show less consciously felt affect of a negative kind, or at least a greater wall of separation between the affect that exists and the underlying danger situation that provoked the symptoms in the absence of adaptive behavior. It might be useful to pursue Freud's implied continuum. Indeed Karl Menninger's use of a continuum model in his unitary theory of mental illness is, among other things, such an attempt.[16] For the present purposes, however, we have gone far enough to see the kind of relationship that Freud felt obtained between affect and anxiety (as signal) when the normative process that should be triggered

43

off by anxiety is dealt with through various degrees and grada-
tions of maladaptation.

When the anxiety signal is heard and proper adaptation is
made in relation to the danger of which it warns, we have seen
that the affect accompanying the point of recognition and initial
action may be high, but that there is little immediate feeling of
"hurt," that the affect after the crisis hurts more, but is tolerable
and temporary since the direction of proper adaptation has been
set, and that the long-term residual of the affect is constructive
because it increases alertness and hence adaptive capacity.

We have also seen that all situations in which the anxiety signal
is not heard and proper adaptation pursued have something in
common about affect, although with a wide difference in degree.
Generally speaking, the thicker the wall between the danger
situation and conscious acceptance of its nature and its dangerous-
ness, the less will be the conscious affect of a constrictive kind.
The psychiatric dilemma is this. The better symptoms work (to
conceal the danger situation), the less appropriate and genuine
the affect, and the more inaccessible the person to therapeutic
measures. But the more constrictive affect increases, the more danger there is that this will paralyze the person, and induce a retreat
into symptoms. All therapies that aim at more than symptomatic
relief may be said, therefore, to operate by increasing the capacity
to tolerate recognition of the danger about which the anxiety
alarm warns—but doing so conservatively—in the recognition
that reversions and regressions are possible at all points.

Our analysis of Freud's view of affect and anxiety has also
brought out another important point: Only persons in whom the
anxiety signal is followed by proper adaptation can regard the
affect induced as temporary. All other persons assume implicitly
that, if they really hear the signal, they will hear it forever. It is
this patterned quality of "foreverness" that is usually held in
mind when anxiety is defined as affect. Persons who have suffered
long periods with severe intermittent physical pain report that
the anticipation of the next stab of pain is more demoralizing
than the moments of acute pain in themselves. The person who

deals nonnormatively with the anxiety signal assumes that, if he should fully heed it, he would feel its acute pain forever—intermittently perhaps, but eternally. The affect he does actually experience consciously is, therefore, itself an attempt to ward off an anticipated permanent constrictive affect. From a strictly logical point of view, this kind of affect is response to an inference. It may be painful with a shocking intensity. And since the pain itself (constrictive affect) is not remedial, effort must be made to relieve it. But the goal is not its complete elimination. Instead the goal is to help the person to view the affect as contemporary and temporary, not as fated (past and future) and forever.

Forms of Anxiety According to Freud's Theory

The distinctions that Freud made between "true" and "neurotic" anxiety and between "objective" and "neurotic" anxiety should be understood in the light of the above discussion.[17] These distinctions are not about two kinds of phenomena both going under the name of "anxiety." They represent, instead, general descriptions of what happens when a capacity of the human being (hearing and heeding danger signals) is used normatively and when it is not. When the whole process of which anxiety is the trigger is appropriate, then anxiety as constrictive affect soon disappears and leaves only improved alertness as its heir. When the overall process in which anxiety is embedded is, however, inappropriate, then there is pathology. But it is not anxiety that has made it so. Neurotic anxiety, we might say, is neurotic not because it is anxiety but because it is neurotic. Less epigrammatically, anxiety gives rise to neurotic affect only when the capacity of the person to hear and heed its message is impaired.

The same caution should be observed in interpreting Freud's distinction among the three "varieties" of anxiety: "objective anxiety, neurotic anxiety, and moral anxiety." [18] These refer to the three different kinds of sources of danger that cause the anxiety signal to be sounded. In all instances "the ego is the only seat of anxiety." [19] When the source of danger sensed by the ego is from the external world, there is objective anxiety. When it is from the id, there is neurotic anxiety. And when from the super-ego, there is moral anxiety.

To say that only the ego (not the id or super-ego) can "produce and feel anxiety" or that the ego is "the only seat of anxiety" is one way of asserting that the whole alarm apparatus of the human person is an aspect of the directive center of personality and is not regulated by some "part process." The distinction of "objective" from "neurotic" and "moral" anxiety, however, shows that the ego is alert to dangers that come from both outside and inside. And the distinction between "neurotic" and "moral" anxiety asserts that the dangers from inside may come either from the primitive drive part of the psyche or from that which has introjected cultural teaching. Since Freud's view of the super-ego shows it, so to speak, as the agent of the outside that operates inside, his "moral" variety of anxiety may be seen as related both to outside and inside. Since the three forms are "varieties" and not entities or even species, they point to the unity underlying the differences—the differences being in terms of the source of danger, and the unity in the process, aim, or function.

When he examined anxiety from a developmental point of view, Freud asked what experiences in early life would give rise to "a condition of increased sensory attention and motor tension." [20]

The emergence of what he called a state of "anxiety-preparedness" he held to be due to certain early universal experiences, beginning with the fact of birth itself, although he rejected Otto Rank's extreme statement of the birth trauma.[21] In boys he felt the fear of castration was important, while in girls there was the "fear of loss of love." [22] After the super-ego develops, another mode of being alerted to danger is provided.

Freud's statements concerning the genetic roots of anxiety have sometimes been interpreted as if they were merely reductionistic in intent. It ought not to be denied that he never rid himself of the reductionistic bias he learned in nineteenth-century science. But in seeking to locate the prototypical experiences out of which "anxiety-preparedness," or the capacity to be alerted, arose, what he was actually doing was two things: First, he was indicating that the potential capacity of the organism to be alerted was native and not reducible to anything else. Second, he was implying that the *content* of what one should be alerted about is learned. As to the second, the attempt to locate the prototypical experiences out of which "anxiety-preparedness" emerges tends to suggest certain universal kinds of dangers about which the whole race learns. But allowance is also made for specifics and for wide degrees of variation, in what will make the alarm ring. For example, even if snakes could be demonstrated to be phallic symbols universally, the signal of alarm given about snakes would be quite different in a region with, as against a region without, poisonous snakes.

It is important to note how little Freud said about the distinction between fear and anxiety. This distinction, which has much obvious commonsense merit, simply notes the difference between a danger a person can identify and one he cannot. In Freud's view, making much of this distinction would tend to obscure the theoretical problem. Ramzy puts this piquantly in his suggestion that only animals and angels can have fear while man has anxiety. This is an indirect way of talking about man's capacity for self-transcendence. Not even an apparently simple danger is read by man automatically, apart from what he has learned from the past and anticipates of the future. Even if the interval between first perception and understanding is infinitesimal, the awareness of danger is always filtered through man's interpretative apparatus. Thus a truer statement of the distinction in human beings between fear and anxiety would be to call the first the alarm signal that is read accurately without perceptible pause between signal and interpretation, while the latter involves perceptible pause. The virtue of these latter definitions is not only their greater accuracy but also their important warning that the coexistence of an objective danger and a constrictive feeling is no necessary indication that the first accounts for the second without remainder.

Freud's Earlier Theories

It is one of the many merits of Ramzy's chapter that he shows the extent to which Freud's final theory of anxiety represented a great shift of perspective from his earlier views. So far our discussion has dealt only with the later theory and its implications. As we have seen, the most important fact about the latter theory is its concentration on defining the function of anxiety and its treatment of affect as consequent upon the extent to, and the way in, which anxiety as a danger signal is perceived and followed up by the ego. Freud's earlier theory or theories, however, still have importance in two ways.

In the first place, the apparent simplicity of the early theories is still taken by many people to be the Freudian understanding of anxiety, perhaps especially by those who have failed to examine the rewarding but complex dialectics of the later theory. It is important to understand the magnificent work that went into Freud's earlier theories, as Ramzy describes so well, in order to appreciate the conviction, the courage, and the revolution that forced him to move to the later theory.

In the second place is the fact that the core idea in Freud's early theory of anxiety is still useful if it is seen for what it is, rather than as a definition of anxiety. Freud's earlier statements were, for example, about "frustrated excitation." [23] If "frustrated excitation" is seen as a specific instance of a more general class of "danger situations," then it is plain, according to the later theory, that an anxiety signal will be given about it. This signal may be heard and heeded, or any of the various kinds of pathology may ensue. Believing, in his early theory, that anxiety *is* affect, Freud wrote, "Anxiety is thus general current coin for which all the affects are exchanged, or can be exchanged, when the corresponding ideational content is under repression." [24] If we substitute in this sentence for the word "anxiety" the phrase, "The response to the alarm signal of danger, in any of its pathological forms," we then have an important insight from the first theory illuminating an aspect of the second. The earlier theory also reminds us that the intensity the ego feels about the nature of the danger

48

conditions markedly the type of response that is possible. This is of considerable clinical significance.

Rollo May and Others on Anxiety

Our discussion has focused upon Freud's understanding of anxiety because it has been focal to all other modern scientific work and thought on this subject. Yet it must be said that much good scientific work has been done since Freud. As Rollo May's summary makes clear, what is most striking is the number of perspectives from which anxiety may fruitfully be examined.[25] Liddell's studies[26] of "vigilance" in animals, Goldstein's investigations[27] of traumatic brain damage, and studies by cultural anthropologists are only some of the significant recent contributions. In relation to anxiety as to other subjects, the tendency of the psychotherapeutic groups, who broke off from psychoanalysis, was to stress the cultural dimensions of the problem. In Sullivan's understanding of anxiety, for example, emphasis is placed upon the interpersonal context from which anxiety arises.[28] It is important, he wrote, "to find the basic vulnerabilities to anxiety in interpersonal relations, rather than to deal with symptoms called out by anxiety or to avoid anxiety." He discusses anxiety in unqualified terms as having "paralyzing power." [29] This is a less dialectical view than Freud's, even though the whole of Sullivan's understanding of anxiety is worth careful study.

Rollo May's view is closer to Freud's than is Sullivan's. May's formal definition is: "Anxiety is the apprehension cued off by a threat to some value which the individual holds essential to his existence as a personality." [30] Functionally speaking, the same general kind of relationship between alarm and affect is contained in this conception as in Freud's. The principal difference is in May's implication that the term "anxiety" should be used only in relation to the alarm rung for a central or focal threat, rather than for all types of danger in all degrees. May's contribution to understanding anxiety, both in his review of other work and in his original study, is significant and worth study. But in defining the function of anxiety, it represents no basic change from Freud.

CONSTRUCTIVE ASPECTS OF ANXIETY

References

1. Rollo May, *The Meaning of Anxiety* (New York: The Ronald Press Company, 1950).
2. Ishak Ramzy and Robert S. Wallerstein et al, "Pain, Fear and Anxiety: A Study in Their Interrelationships," *Psychoanalytic Study of the Child* (New York: International Universities Press, Inc., 1958), XIII, 147-89.
3. Sigmund Freud, *New Introductory Lectures on Psycho-Analysis*, trans. W. J. H. Sprott (New York: W. W. Norton and Company, Inc., 1933). Used by permission. P. 128.
4. *Ibid.*
5. Freud, "Inhibitions, Symptoms and Anxiety," *Standard Edition of the Complete Psychological Works of Sigmund Freud*, general ed. and trans. James Strachey (24 vols.; New York: The Macmillan Co., 1961). Used by permission of The Hogarth Press and Basic Books, Inc. XX, 87-174.
6. *Ibid.*
7. *Ibid.*
8. Freud, *A General Introduction to Psychoanalysis (Introductory Lectures on Psychoanalysis)*, ed. and trans. Joan Riviere (Garden City: Permabooks, Inc., 1949), p. 404.
9. *Ibid.* See the important comments on etymology by Outler in chap. IV.
10. Freud, *New Introductory Lectures*, p. 114.
11. *Ibid.*
12. *Ibid.*, p. 115.
13. Freud, "Analysis of a Phobia in a Five-Year-Old Boy," *Standard Edition*, X, 5-149.
14. Freud, *New Introductory Lectures*, p. 115.
15. *Ibid.*
16. This theory is explained in *The Vital Balance* to be published in 1963 by The Viking Press.
17. Freud, "Inhibitions, Symptoms and Anxiety," *Standard Edition*, XX, 165.
18. *Ibid.*
19. *Ibid.*, p. 118.
20. *Ibid.*, p. 114.
21. *Ibid.*, p. 122 ff.
22. *Ibid.*, p. 121.
23. Freud, *A General Introduction*, p. 408.
24. *Ibid.*, pp. 410-11.
25. May, *op. cit.*, Part I.
26. Howard Liddell, "The Role of Vigilance in the Development of Animal Neurosis," *Anxiety*, eds. P. H. Hoch and Joseph Zubin (New York: Grune & Stratton, Inc., 1950).
27. Kurt Goldstein, *The Organism* (New York: American Book Company, 1939).
28. Harry S. Sullivan, *The Interpersonal Theory of Psychiatry*, eds. H. S. Perry and M. L. Gawel (New York: W. W. Norton and Company, Inc., 1953), p. 11.
29. *Ibid.*
30. May, *op. cit.*, p. 191.

"Anxiety is an expression for the perfection [making valid] of human nature."

—SÖREN KIERKEGAARD

"Anxiety is the precondition of sin."

—REINHOLD NIEBUHR

"Anxiety is the existential awareness of nonbeing."

—PAUL TILLICH

CHAPTER III

Some Theories of Anxiety: Theological

Seward Hiltner

This chapter continues the description of three comprehensive theories of anxiety of which the first, that of Freud, appeared in the previous chapter. Here we shall present the view of Sören Kierkegaard and as associated with it the understanding of Reinhold Niebuhr. We shall conclude with an account of Paul Tillich's theory of anxiety.

The reader should note that this chapter is no more a complete history of theological views of anxiety than the previous chapter was a thorough history of psychiatric views of anxiety. Both kinds of history would be valuable, and both need to be written; but they are far beyond our scope or our competence. Attention, however, is called especially to chap. V by Albert C. Outler with its exposition of the views of Augustine on anxiety. Certainly no point of view about this topic is more important in Christian history than that of Augustine.

Sören Kierkegaard's Theory

Kierkegaard, who lived in Denmark a bit more than a century ago, was the first modern theologian to deal seriously with anxiety. Usually now regarded as the father of modern existentialism, Kierkegaard was a relentless attacker of the prevailing Hegelian "system," and was thus a precursor of Freud in taking seriously the factors of life that cannot neatly be encompassed in conscious and rational schemes of interpretation.[1]

Unlike his treatment of many other subjects, Kierkegaard devoted an entire book to anxiety.[2] Provided one understands the general context of his thought in which anxiety finds its place, therefore, the explicit consideration of anxiety may be pursued mainly through this volume, *The Concept of Dread*.

Kierkegaard's consideration of anxiety emerges out of his questions concerning original sin. Sin to Kierkegaard is what separates man from God and therefore what also separates him from becoming what he ought to become. It is especially important in understanding Kierkegaard to get rid of the moralistic notion that sin is either evil deeds done by a few wicked men or naughty ones done by everybody. Sin can be understood only in relation to God. Sin is meaningless except in a context in which God is made explicit. If sin is "talked about as a sickness, an abnormality, a poison, a disharmony," it has already been subverted.[3]

Sin is the condition of every actual man before God. Yet it is not an automatic accompaniment of man's humanness. The critical questions Kierkegaard posed, therefore, were: How does sin get started? What is the prototype of sin? Whether the question is asked about the human race or the human person, what is the "original sin"? As Kierkegaard himself put the problem, "The first sin is a determinant of quality, the first sin is *the* sin." [4] What happens when this "first sin" takes place?

Kierkegaard's answer was that the prototypical sin comes about through anxiety. Anxiety is recognition of "the reality of freedom as possibility anterior to possibility." [5] So long as man, or a man, is in a state of "innocence" in which his "spirit" (which means his true nature including his freedom) is "dreaming," he cannot be said to be either sinful or free.[6] But once he begins to look at his true situation as a human being, continuation of the ignorant "innocence" is no longer possible. He sees that his freedom is real, that it contains possibility or potentiality (rather than a clearly marked course) , and that he therefore bears responsibility for what is done with his freedom. This is his wakening as "spirit" (free and responsible) from his "dreaming."

In describing this confrontation with the "possibility anterior to possibility," Kierkegaard talked of the "abyss" in suggesting what it is that man looks at. He spoke of "dizziness" to connote man's feelings while looking at it.[7] "One may liken anxiety to dizziness. He whose eye chances to look down into the yawning abyss becomes dizzy. But the reason for it is just as much his eye as it is the precipice."[8] The very act of looking, in other words, shows the viewer that he has already made some kind of choice within the whole range of possibility. At this point "freedom then gazes down into its own possibility," and "in this dizziness freedom succumbs."[9] The awareness that one has already made some choice because he has looked down makes him realize, in a more general sense, that he is a choice-making creature whether he wants to be or not. He is like the man in the car (in the previous chapter) who has successfully negotiated the dangerous bridge, who now retrospectively realizes the extent and significance of his choice as he did not at the moment of crisis. And when this general point is projected into the future, with all its implications for all the responsibility of all the choices yet to be made, then in "this dizziness freedom succumbs," and one draws back.

To Kierkegaard, freedom and anxiety are two sides of the same coin. To look seriously at freedom is to confront the infinity of possibility, "which does not tempt like a definite choice, but alarms and fascinates."[10] It is the quality connoted by alarm and fascination that makes one dizzy. And in view of the real nature of this alarm plus fascination (which is a proper rendition of the actual situation), one *ought* to feel dizzy when he confronts it. At this point, however, there enters Kierkegaard's equivalent of pathology. One is gravely tempted to try to avoid the dizziness. If he can succeed in denying that possibility is as wide as it really is or that he has responsibility for decisions about it or that he has any genuine freedom or that he is guilty if he uses freedom wrongly, then he can avoid direct and painful feelings of the dizziness.

If there is no freedom, there can be no sin. And since anxiety (the alarm and fascination) is the inevitable subjective response to confronting the reality of freedom and possibility, the connection between anxiety and sin is very close.[11] Once the whole process gets under way—movement from innocence, awareness that one has chosen, consciousness of the immense range of choice, alarm and fascination in the face of this dizziness, temptation to retreat—then anxiety about sin itself produces sin.[12] Through this whole process, sin via anxiety feeds on itself and perpetuates itself.

To Kierkegaard, what is the normative or proper way to end this process? If temptation arises, how is it to be overcome or eliminated? His answer begins with the implication that the entire process, up to the point of temptation in the above list of stages, cannot be bypassed. There is no answer in a fixation at any prior point in the process, such as the stage of dreamy innocence. Even the "dizziness" is necessary. But when the dizziness comes and with it the temptation to retreat in one way or another, then, Kierkegaard argues, Christian faith teaches us to move through the dizziness, acknowledge and recognize the frightening character of our freedom, and admit our sin. Our ability to move through temptation in this way, despite the attendant pain, may be increased if we recognize that anxiety "is an expression for the perfection of human nature." [13] In more modern language, if man lacked the capacity to see the meaning of possibility and feel the normally resultant dizziness, he would be less than human. To confront and move through anxiety, therefore, is strength. Conversely "the fall into sin always occurs in impotence." [14] For the essence of sin, behaviorally speaking, is retreating before the dizziness brought by the prospect of freedom and its attendant responsibility.

Anxiety is then the painful dizziness in the face of the abyss of possibility. Its function in human life, when it is involved in a total normative concrete process, is to compel us to accept ourselves as "spirit" as well as "nature," that is, as responsible, imaginative, creative, and free beings who cannot pretend that we live as do animals even though we are animals also. As the capacity for feeling the dizziness, anxiety is man's uniquely human possession; for without it he would not be imaginative, and so on. But as painfully subjective feeling, anxiety is two-edged and ambiguous. The pain *always* is a *temptation* to retreat, and in most men there is yielding to the temptation.

While the normative function in human life that anxiety is present to perform is constructive, this is very far from saying that anxiety always, or even very often, appears within a total concrete process that enables the normative function to be performed. More often than not there is retreat from anxiety, from freedom, from responsibility, and from the acknowledgment of sin. All this is the pathology of anxiety, as we might now put it. But it is not the *fault* of *anxiety*. To be sure, the retreat was triggered by the painful dizziness. But it was the person's inability to confront and move through the dizziness that produced the retreat, not the dizziness in itself. What was at fault was the self's inability to sustain the pain of the dizziness, not the anxiety itself. By implication, to study the pathology of anxiety is to examine the forces that prevent the self from confronting the dizziness and instead permit it to retreat.

From Kierkegaard's point of view, if there were no capacity for anxiety there would be no capacity for creativity either. But this is very different from saying that anxiety is the basis of creativity or that there is no creativity without anxiety. Unless man could look at freedom, possibility, and his responsibility for choice within them, he could not create in the proper sense of the term. But since looking at freedom always rightly brings the dizziness of anxiety, in that sense anxiety must be moved through if actual creativity is to take place. The same capacity that makes it possible for man subjectively to feel dizzy before the abyss may, if he moves through it, enable him to be creative. But any statement professing to make anxiety as an affect the necessary cause of or ingredient in creativity would distort Kierkegaard's view.

Since Kierkegaard's interest and concern were manifestly not clinical, we cannot find in him a pathological typology that is directly comparable to Freud's. He was not, however, without typologies. And it might be possible to use his categories of religious, moral, and aesthetic (all defined very idiosyncratically) as increasing degrees of pathological response to the alarm and fascination of anxiety. They might be put on a continuum. But for our purposes, the thing to be noted is that there are wrong ways in which anxiety may be responded to and that these far outnumber the occasions on which the whole process in which the person is engaged does come to normative fruition "for the perfection of human nature."

When the question of the normative function of anxiety in human life is put in the foreground, therefore, it becomes plain, according to our analysis, that Freud and Kierkegaard are much closer together than their widely divergent general concerns would lead us to believe. Both see anxiety performing its normative function when a signal of danger is heard or a prod to move in a new way is heeded. Both suggest that the alarm or prod in itself is not determinative of the outcome of the whole process. Both see the pain or negative affect, when the process works normatively, as giving rise to an attitude or outlook that Pruyser helpfully calls "cognitive." [15] Both recognize a pathology of anxiety, the forms of which may be placed on a continuum model, but this is spelled out only by Freud. Clinical affect—that is, affect when the process in which anxiety is involved has not operated normatively—is discussed only by Freud. Generally speaking then Pruyser is right in suggesting that affect in the clinical sense is not much involved in Kierkegaard's view of anxiety, while it is plainly important in Freud's.[16]

It would be equally false to Freud and to Kierkegaard to say that anxiety is constructive or to say that it is destructive. Both would say that the intent of anxiety is constructive; that is, the purpose for which man possesses the signaling or prodding apparatus is constructive. But whether it is constructive or destructive in outcome depends upon the response made and executed by ego, self, or person. If the intensity of the person's affect is such that he is paralyzed or retreats, then what concretely follows is negative and destructive. But if it is said that the "anxiety" is destructive, then it should be understood that this refers to the affect in the process where anxiety has already failed to perform its normative function.

Reinhold Niebuhr's Theory

The view of anxiety held by Reinhold Niebuhr, one of the best-known American theologians of today, is almost identical with that of Kierkegaard, though their views and even interests differ widely on some other matters. Niebuhr's concern about anxiety, like that of Kierkegaard, emerges out of his consideration of sin.[17] Sin is failing to accept one's freedom and the responsibility that goes along with it and, at the same time, the limits of that freedom. Sin takes two basic forms, as Niebuhr sees it, pride and sensuality. Pride is acting as if one were more than he is, as if he had no limits. Sensuality is retreat from the responsibilities that accompany freedom. When we say that man is free, we mean that he is self-transcendent, capable of looking and moving beyond himself. Man, however, is also finite and limited. He is neither animal nor angel, and he cannot treat his biological nature as if it made him only an animal nor his self-transcendence as if it made him a god. If and when he does either of these things, he is committing one of the two forms of sin.

Being both free and finite, Niebuhr continues, man is inevitably anxious. "Anxiety is the inevitable concomitant of the paradox of freedom and finiteness in which man is involved." [18] It is the inevitable or necessary response, like Kierkegaard's dizziness, to a recognition of man's true situation. The anxiety, that is, is inevitable. Man's responses to it may differ. But in Niebuhr's view they never differ sufficiently to prevent the movement from anxiety to sin. "Yet anxiety is not sin." [19] And although "anxiety is the internal precondition of sin," the inevitable presence of anxiety may not be used, Niebuhr argues, to take the responsibility of sin away from man.[20]

A man is tempted to sin, that is, to set himself above his proper limits (pride) or to deny his spiritual nature by sinking back into unlimited devotion to limited values (sensuality).[21] Anxiety is to be seen as the internal dimension of what, when viewed externally, is "temptation." But that which tempts or tries us may, depending upon our response to it, lead in either of two directions. On the one hand, it is possible that "creativity" may emerge from the confrontation with temptation and anxiety, and on the other, that sin may appear.[22] Niebuhr is suspicious that the absence of anxiety altogether would also mean the failure to confront freedom, even though he holds that faith is designed to come to terms with anxiety.[23]

For Niebuhr then the outcome of anxiety is indeterminate. But the capacity for anxiety is an aspect of man's self-transcendence. It is "precondition" of and corollary with man's capacities for both sin and creativity. But whether sin or creativity will emerge is not given in the nature of the anxiety itself.

Since Niebhur, unlike Kierkegaard, is a contemporary and in addition knows much about the social and psychological sciences, we might expect his discussion of anxiety to include a clinical dimension. On the whole he disappoints us here. In some of his writings he does indicate the importance of psychiatric and related therapies for some people, generally regarding these as just the people who are most lacking in genuine human freedom (and of course, therefore, in capacity for sin). But even with these people he makes the point that if their therapy increases their freedom, so it will increase their *capacity* for sin. Niebuhr wants no one to rest on his oars. Shrewdly he argues that the most dangerous oar-resters are the good people, the free people, the moral people, the healthy people; for these very qualities may lead to sin in the form of pride, and if they do, the resulting damage is greater than in the case of the less good, the less free, the less moral, or the less healthy. The better or freer or healthier a man is, the more it behooves him to have enough uneasiness so as not to become proud. Niebuhr sometimes calls this uneasiness "anxiety."

Except in approving psychiatric therapy for the unfree who need it, Niebuhr does not discuss the affect of or about anxiety. Nor is he always careful to distinguish the capacity to experience anxiety from the subjective affect of feeling it. When he indicates that temptation—and its internal dimension of anxiety—may lead to either creativity or sin, he is assuming that there is some freedom of choice in the response, which means at minimum that the person is not paralyzed. A systematic statement of his theory would seem to require him to make this distinction clear. He would probably then say that when anxiety performs its normative function it is embedded in a total process in which there is sufficient freedom of the person to be able to avoid sin, whether the decision is made against sin in actuality or not. In his eagerness, however, to retain the free and self-transcendent powers of the self in all possible conditions, Niebuhr sometimes suggests some odd statistics.[24] He has sometimes written as if only a handful of people had their freedom significantly impaired, while the overwhelming majority have enough core freedom to make decisions in the face of temptation. His emphasis is certainly a message to the relatively free and healthy. It may underestimate the number who lack freedom and are handicapped by unhealthy attitudes.

As in Kierkegaard, the affect that Niebuhr associates with anxiety is not clinically paralyzing, and again Pruyser's analysis of it as "cognitive state" is helpful.[25] To be sure, some kind of negative affect is assumed as the internal dimension of temptation, unless one simply acquiesces. But this is conceived to be a shifting of values, a putting of oneself in one's place, so to speak. What Niebuhr underestimates is the number of persons whose fall into sin, upon confronting temptation, comes about through a paralysis owing not to freedom but to the compulsion of prior experience. Nevertheless we may note that on the understanding of the normative function of the total process of which anxiety is a part, Niebuhr is identical with Kierkegaard. And we have suggested that, on the central points, Kierkegaard agrees with Freud.

Paul Tillich's Theory

The context in which Paul Tillich's understanding of anxiety is set is a bit different from that of Kierkegaard and Niebuhr. It is more explicitly philosophical in that it begins from a concern for ontology, the understanding of being. In the general sense, anxiety to Tillich is to be understood as "the state in which a being is aware of its possible nonbeing," or "anxiety is the existential awareness of nonbeing." [26] If some part of its object is accurately known, then anxiety may be modified. But the real object of true anxiety "is the negation of every object." [27] Indeed anxiety drives the person to try "to establish objects of fear." [28] But the fact is that "the basic anxiety, the anxiety of a finite being about the threat of nonbeing, cannot be eliminated" whether by attempting to objectivize it or in some other way.[29]

In its root meaning then Tillich holds anxiety to be existential in character. Thus even though anxiety may always be related to the possibility of nonbeing, the forms that it may assume for different persons or cultures or in different periods of history may vary according to whatever is the greatest threat to existence. Taking a long look at the history of Western civilization, Tillich suggests that the dominant form of anxiety was different at three critical periods. At the time of the break-up of Greek civilization, anxiety threatened man relatively in terms of fate and absolutely in terms of death.[30] At the time of the Reformation, the relative form was guilt, while the absolute form was condemnation.[31] In our day anxiety appears relatively as emptiness and absolutely as meaninglessness.[32] These three forms, Tillich makes clear, are to be understood as relative emphases, not categorical such that one excludes the others. Tillich regards them as accurate representations of the threats that were and are crucial to man's existence in each of the three periods named.

Tillich makes explicit acknowledgment of an anxiety gone wrong, not helping us to meet and confront the basic threat to our existence in whatever cultural or historical or personal form it appears to us. This he calls either "pathological anxiety" or "neurotic anxiety." [33] Eager not to appear to say that the anxiety gone wrong is thereby not anxiety as previously defined, Tillich writes, "Pathological anxiety is a state of existential anxiety under special conditions." [34] It has gone wrong because it is "the result of contingent occurrences in human life." [35] Anxiety in its neurotic or pathological forms differs from "existential anxiety" most sharply in the way it should be handled. It is "illness and danger and must be healed," while existential anxiety is to be dealt with through confrontation.[36] Pathological anxiety does, however, contain some ambiguity. By threatening the break-up of old patterns, it may under proper conditions be a stimulus to creativity. The fact is that the average person, in Tillich's view, avoids both existential and neurotic anxiety, but he does so at the price of creativity.[37]

Tillich's calling for "a sharp distinction between existential and pathological anxiety" is for the practical reason that the latter is to be healed and the former, confronted.[38] This does not contradict the statement that pathological anxiety is existential anxiety under special conditions. Since Tillich does not articulate the special conditions, the full intent of his argument here is not clear. But the impression gained is that pathological anxiety arises when one has been unable to evade the confrontation with existential anxiety by becoming just "average" and yet has not been able to do the confronting either. It is extremely doubtful that Tillich means, by this part of his argument, that an inoculation of confronting existential anxiety makes one immune to pathological anxiety, although some of his theological readers read him in the light of such a psychiatric insurance policy.

To use Pruyser's term, the "cognitive" trend in Tillich's understanding of anxiety is shown most clearly in this general definition, "Anxiety is the awareness of unsolved conflicts between structural elements of the personality." [39] The structural elements are illustrated as follows:

Conflicts between unconscious drives and repressive norms, between drives trying to dominate the center of the personality, between imaginary worlds and the experience of the real world, between trends toward greatness and perfection and the experience of one's smallness and imperfection, between the desire to be accepted by other people or society or the universe and the experience of being rejected, between the will to be and the seemingly intolerable burden of being which evokes the open or hidden desire not to be.[40]

It should be noted that this list moves from the intrapsychic through the interpersonal toward the ontological level. Precisely which of these are to be "solved" by healing and which by confrontation, Tillich does not specify. But the statement beginning "Anxiety is the awareness of" suggests that the first step in dealing with all forms of anxiety is an "awareness." This makes Tillich's theory different from those of Freud, Kierkegaard, and Niebuhr. For it extends anxiety beyond the function of alarm or prod to include the reception or awareness of what is being warned or prodded about. It is this extension that enables Tillich to think of even pathological anxiety as not only a warning of what is wrong but also as itself the first move toward putting it right. This position opens Tillich to the possible charge of reifying anxiety, as if it were a concrete process in itself, rather than viewing it as a factor within a larger concrete process as do Freud, Kierkegaard, and Niebuhr.

Although all anxiety to Tillich has some affect of "painful feeling," existential anxiety is not to be understood as a continuing stage of high or intense feeling.[41] Tillich's illustration is, "We are not always aware of our having to die, but in the light of the experience of our having to die our whole life is experienced differently." [42] Anxiety as "despair is not always" or steadily "present. But the rare occasions in which it is present determine the interpretation of existence as a whole." [43] In more psychological language, the confrontation leads toward an attitude of alertness with certain specific content, but not to paralysis or to a continuation of high emotion in the physiological sense.

The normative course of existential anxiety occurs when man takes it "courageously . . . unto himself." [44] Rational consequences should follow confrontation with each of the three main forms that existential anxiety assumes. In confronting the anxiety of fate and death, men may try to develop means for their safety and protection; however, in case their attempt to do so becomes a compulsive clutch at absolute and final security, then the response has become pathological. In dealing with the guilt and condemnation form of anxiety, men may avoid guilty responsibility by avoiding actions that will lead to it. But this may become distorted into some kind of perfectionism.[45] The anxiety of emptiness and meaninglessness, which Tillich believes focal in our time, should lead toward interpretations of life that do give meaning. But if this turns into a compulsive quest for absolute certainty, then its purpose is lost and it has become pathological.[46]

If we were to ask Tillich his view of the normative function of anxiety, he would reply in terms of its trying to make us aware of the threats to our existence in whatever form is most relevant to us or to our age. This implies not only a message but also the beginnings of empowerment. We regard this latter implication with suspicion. Our other three authors all agree, against Tillich, that what makes confrontation possible is not the message of anxiety itself but something else, such as strength of ego or freedom of the self. To all of them, the initial pain of receiving the message is more clearly noted than in Tillich. In terms of Pruyser's distinction between anxiety as affect and as cognitive state, it is most notably the second in Tillich.

Tillich's attempt to make his theory of anxiety an integrated one is seen principally in his effort to include pathological anxiety either as a form of existential anxiety ("existential anxiety under special conditions") or to see the pathological and existential as forms of anxiety in general ("the awareness of unsolved conflicts between structural elements of the personality"). The former way of putting it tends to build from the top down instead of from the bottom up (as in Freud and to some extent also in Kierkegaard and Niebuhr), while the latter tends to stress awareness at the expense of affect and may even be misleading at the clinical level. Since Tillich has made no pretensions about the latter, he should not be commented on negatively for the omission. But on a simple descriptive level, an integrated theory of anxiety that is to be both theoretically tenable and clinically useful must do something that Tillich has not attempted.

References

1. For an excellent introductory selection from Kierkegaard's many writings, see *A Kierkegaard Anthology*, ed. Robert Bretall (Princeton: Princeton University Press, 1947).

2. Sören Kierkegaard, *The Concept of Dread,* trans. Walter Lowrie (Princeton: Princeton University Press, 1944). Used by permission. Walter Lowrie's translation of "dread" should have been "anxiety."

3. *Ibid.,* p. 14.

4. *Ibid.,* p. 27.

5. *Ibid.,* p. 38.

6. *Ibid.,* pp. 32, 37.

7. *Ibid.,* p. 55.

8. *Ibid.*

9. *Ibid.*

10. *Ibid.*

11. *Ibid.,* p. 47.

12. *Ibid.,* p. 65.

13. *Ibid.* Here the phrase "for the perfection of" means "making valid," as interpreted to us by a Kierkegaard authority, T. M. Fitzpatrick of the University of Chicago.

14. *Ibid.,* p. 55.

15. See chap. VII.

16. *Ibid.*

17. Reinhold Niebuhr, *The Nature and Destiny of Man; A Christian Interpretation* (2 vols.; New York: Charles Scribner's Sons, 1941). I, ch. VII.

18. *Ibid.,* p. 182.

19. *Ibid.,* p. 183.

20. *Ibid.,* p. 182.

21. *Ibid.,* p. 185.

22. *Ibid.*

23. *Ibid.,* p. 183.

24. Niebuhr, *The Self and the Dramas of History* (New York: Charles Scribner's Sons, 1955).

25. See chap. VII.

26. Paul Tillich, *The Courage to Be* (New Haven: Yale University Press, 1952). Used by permission. P. 35.

27. *Ibid.,* p. 36.

28. *Ibid.,* p. 39.

29. *Ibid.*

30. *Ibid.,* p. 41.

31. *Ibid.*

32. *Ibid.*

33. *Ibid.,* p. 65.

34. *Ibid.*

35. *Ibid.,* p. 64.

36. *Ibid.,* p. 69.

37. *Ibid.,* pp. 68-69.

38. *Ibid.,* p. 72.

39. *Ibid.,* p. 64.

40. *Ibid.,* pp. 64-65.

41. *Ibid.,* p. 38.

42. *Ibid.,* p. 56.

43. *Ibid.,* pp. 56-57.

44. *Ibid.,* p. 66.

45. *Ibid.,* p. 75.

46. *Ibid.,* p. 76.

"His morbid anxiety . . . corresponded to repressed longing . . ."

—SIGMUND FREUD

"The friendship of the Lord is for those who fear him."

—Ps. 25:14 R.S.V.

CHAPTER IV

Anxious Longing

Fred Berthold, Jr.

Neurotic and Creative Anxiety

The popular existentialists of the postwar period spread abroad, though they also corrupted, Heidegger's contention, stated in *Sein und Zeit,* that *anxiety* provides perhaps the best mirror in which to see human nature.[1] About the same time, in his *Hemmung, Symptom und Angst,* Sigmund Freud stated that anxiety is the central problem of the neuroses.[2]

If indeed anxiety, when read aright, tells us much about human nature, just what does it tell? Novelists and poets, philosophers and theologians, as well as psychiatrists, have all taken their turn at trying to read the enigma. We would do well at the outset of this essay to remind ourselves that one of the most patient and skilled interpreters of human anxiety, Sigmund Freud, felt until the end of his life a certain bafflement in his efforts to understand anxiety.

At the risk of oversimplifying, I wish to suggest that there are two fundamental perspectives from which the phenomenon of anxiety has been viewed. Further I wish to explore one of these approaches in some detail. And I must end with a confession that it is difficult to see how these two perspectives can be united in a single theory.

Anxiety is properly viewed from the perspective of the clinician or counselor, whose task it is to help a very anxious person. When seen in this context, anxiety often appears to be disteleological—a hindrance to a productive and happy life. Fear is usually teleological; it prepares us to meet or flee from a certain danger. Freud also states that there is such a thing as "real anxiety" or "normal anxiety"—aroused not so much by a specific threatening object as by a total danger situation. But anxiety as the clinician sees it is often "neurotic," out of proportion to any real danger situation. Rather than preparing the individual for fight or flight, it seems simply to disorient him. He feels threatened by a vague something which he cannot even locate much less deal with. Or in cases where the anxiety is tied to a specific object, it seems so overwhelming as to rob the person of any powers of judgment or action.

Concerning anxiety as it appears within the clinical context and concerning the strategies of treatment, I have little to say, since I am in these respects a complete layman. Nevertheless there are two assumptions which I shall make without which the following analysis must appear questionable or entirely mistaken. First, I assume that a quantitative factor must be taken into account. It may well be, as I shall seek to show, that there is a creative aspect of anxiety, but this disappears when a certain intensity is reached. Many processes, healthy enough in themselves, become destructive when their intensity goes beyond a certain point; for example, anger. Second, I assume that it is legitimate to distinguish between a mental state as immediately felt and its "meaning" within some more comprehensive theory of human nature. This is, of course, taken for granted by depth psychology. Thus a mental state that on the surface has all the characteristics of love may, when other relevant factors are taken into consideration, be revealed as an expression of repressed hostility; and this dynamic love-hate pattern may yield insights into the structure of human personality.

Anxiety has also been viewed from the perspective of the pedagogue; this is, of anyone who feels concerned with improving the human lot vis-à-vis knowledge or justice or God. Those, such as Kierkegaard or Heidegger, who have considered anxiety primarily as a constructive force exemplify this general perspective.[3] They do not necessarily overlook the dreadful aspects of anxiety—and indeed often describe its manifest content in the same terms as the clinician. But within all this they see an "anxiety to . . ." They read the signs as tokens of a desire to better one's lot and imply that without anxiety there would be no impetus to learning or improvement. Knowledge, in this connection, is the transformation of anxiety into fear—the identification of *what* is "wrong." But anxiety is the mother of the drive to know.

I wish to argue that this second perspective is more inclusive, that the kind of crippling anxieties, which are daily observed by the clinician, are special cases of the more basic phenomenon. More specifically I feel that anxiety is fundamentally a creative element in man's life, that it is a "child of love." This is by no means to say that morbid anxieties are always in practice reversible. Analogously a sexual perversion is, I think, inexplicable without reference to the normal and creative development of sexual life. But in a particular case all kinds of circumstances may make it unlikely that the perversion will be overcome. Nevertheless the anxiety of the pervert about his perversion testifies that healthy or normal impulses are still battling for expression.

When we see before our eyes all the overt symptoms of an intense neurotic anxiety, we may well judge it to be in this particular case morbid and disteleological. But this should not prevent us from seeing that anxiety fundamentally has a broader and more creative *meaning* in the total economy of man's life.

My contention—that anxiety is fundamentally and most comprehensively an aspect of the creativity of man—can, I believe, be supported from two sides, one psychoanalytic and the other religious. The former I shall discuss only briefly; the latter I wish to enlarge upon somewhat.

Freud's View of Anxiety

Freud's *Problem of Anxiety*[4] does not, so far as I am able as a layman to judge, annul his earlier work on anxiety, but it brings it into a wider and more fruitful context. From this text we learn:

Anxiety is an awareness of a threat; and, dynamically speaking, the threat is equivalent to a threat of separation from the loved object.

The importance of the relation to the loved object comes out clearly in the following passage. "Hans woke up one morning in tears. Asked why he was crying, he said to his mother: "When I was asleep, I thought you were gone, and I had no mummy to coax with (caress)." Freud comments:

> The disorder set in with thoughts which were *at the same time fearful and sentimental,* and then followed an anxiety dream on the subject of losing his mother and so not being able to coax with her any more. His affection for his mother must therefore have become enormously intensified. This was the fundamental phenomenon in his condition. . . . It was this increased affection for his mother which turned suddenly into anxiety. . . .
>
> His morbid anxiety, then, corresponded to *repressed longing.* . . . He was with his mother and yet he still suffered from anxiety, that is to say, from an *unsatisfied longing* for her.[5]

It is quite clear that Freud regarded this longing as an essential element of anxiety.

> The loved person would not cease to love us nor should we be theatened with castration if we did not entertain certain feelings and intentions within us. Thus, such instinctual impulses are determinants of external dangers and so become dangerous in themselves; and we can now proceed against the external danger by taking measures against the internal ones.[6]

So long as Hans's anxiety remained fixed upon fear of castration (which was expressed in this case as a fear of horses), it was neurotic, crippling, and restrictive. But it is precisely the task of analysis to see beneath the surface to the dynamic meaning of the anxiety. And when this is done, the polarity of anxiety appears. The anxiety about horses is to be understood only within the context of his anxiety to be united with his mother. That which is fearful is fearful only because it threatens the fulfillment of a positive desire. Further when we see Hans's anxiety also in the context of his relation to his father, we see that, for Hans, his phobia represented his effort to come to terms with his situation without renouncing, any more than he felt he had to, the objects of his desire.

The Religious View of Anxiety

When we examine anxiety as it appears in religious experience, we find, I believe, the same sort of dynamic polarity as we find in Freud's view. This may be illustrated by the concept of "the fear of the Lord," which appears again and again in the Bible.

What do you make of the following passage, which refers to the moment when the people of Israel stood before the mountain of God, receiving the Ten Commandments?

And all the people saw the thunderings, and the lightnings, and the noise of the trumpet, and the mountain smoking: and when the people saw it, they removed, and stood afar off. And they said unto Moses, Speak thou with us, and we will hear: but let not God speak with us, lest we die.

And Moses said unto the people, Fear not: for God is come to prove you, and that his fear may be before your faces, that ye sin not. And the people stood afar off, and Moses drew near unto the thick darkness where God was. (Exo. 20:18-21.)

The word used in the injunction not to fear and the word which speaks of that fear which will stop us from sinning are the same except the one is a verb and the other a noun. Both are forms of the Hebrew *yare*.

It is obvious that we have here both threat and blessing. God will prove us, and that prospect is frightening enough to deter us from sin; yet we are not to fear, for somehow this is a gift enabling us to become the children of the covenant, the sons of him who by his steadfast love brought us out of bondage.

Many citations could be given from the Psalms indicating, in various ways, this same duality. Let three instances suffice.

73

Serve the Lord with fear,
  with trembling kiss his feet,
lest he be angry, and you perish in the way;
  for his wrath is quickly kindled.

(Ps. 2:11-12 R.S.V.)

I through the abundance of thy steadfast love
  will enter thy house,
I will worship toward thy holy temple
  in the fear of thee.

(Ps. 5:7 R.S.V.)

The friendship of the Lord is for those who fear him,
  and he makes known to them his covenant.

(Ps. 25:14 R.S.V.)

There is fear of the Lord in the sense of the fear of his wrath and punishment, but also fear in the sense of reverence and desire for his "friendship." In biblical religion there is the threat of separation, because of sin, from the loved object. This threat, with its polar aspects of desire for God and threat of separation, is reflected in the concept of the "fear of the Lord."

The few citations I have given, from Freud and from the Bible, can hardly establish my thesis concerning the relation of anxiety to the creative side of human life. Nor could it be shown, even by more extended references, that these authors really meant to say what I am saying. I want to argue for a view which goes beyond what they have said explicitly. Yet I feel that my view is suggested by and compatible with the literature to which I have referred. But a hint of this must suffice, for I wish to use the bulk of my chapter on a more constructive effort. There are three basic aspects of religious experience with relation to which anxiety typically appears. I want to show how, in connection with each, my basic thesis is supported.

It would no doubt be desirable to state a general theory of anxiety and to show how the phenomena to which I shall refer fit into the theory, perhaps as modes or types of anxiety. Unfortunately I do not find sufficient clarity either in the literature or in my own thoughts to accomplish this. Nevertheless it seems to me that viewing anxiety in the context of the creative development of the individual and seeing neurotic anxiety as a special case within this broad framework helps to carry our inquiry forward. My task is to show how this may be so in connection with certain very pervasive aspects of religious experience.

So far as the present paper is concerned, it makes no difference whether or not the theological categories might be ultimately reducible to psychological ones. I am concerned with the structure of anxiety as it appears in certain phenomena, not with the ontological status of the objects referred to by the religious man.

Radical Freedom and the Anxiety of Creativity

One aspect of religious experience that is relevant to our topic has been treated by Sören Kierkegaard.[7] According to him, the Bible depicts man as a creature (with the limitations that express themselves in ignorance and death) who is yet a creator (shaping his world and his future). The juxtaposition of these elements gives rise to the *anxiety of creativity*. Man is *anxious to* shape his future, but he is also *anxious about* the threats that may lurk in the abyss of the unknown and other seemingly infinite possibilities, which are opaque to his finite mind. Given the conditions of human existence, the fundamental anxiety of creativity is dialectically related to the anxiety of dread.

In working this out, Kierkegaard goes back to Adamic myth, and I should like to do this too, because I think that in this way one can see that the text is not being just forced or manipulated.[8]

According to Genesis, Adam is given a very sweeping mandate: "Be fruitful and multiply, and fill the earth and subdue it; and have dominion . . ." (1:28 R.S.V.) Is this the prologue to *Dr. Faustus?* No, it is the Bible. Man is in a very real sense to participate in the creation of his world; one might almost say he is to be the "god of this world," for it is the prerogative of God to have dominion. In short, man is placed in a situation of radical freedom. I speak of freedom not in the sense of absence of causation,

75

whatever that might mean. Of such speculations the Bible is innocent. I speak of freedom in the sense of *possibility,* of a future that man has a role in shaping.

We next learn that man faces the future, with all its possibilities, in ignorance. (Gen. 1:5-6.) Specifically he is ignorant of good and evil, that is of what his choices may bring in the way of fulfillment or frustration. Man has freedom, but he feels the lack of wisdom, of guidance, of security in knowing the consequences of his choices. Of course, the Bible no doubt wishes to imply that this ignorance is no cause for despair, since man has God and faith to guide him. But from a human perspective—is not the openness of the future alarming without knowledge in advance of how it will all come out? Man has the exhilaration of "being able . . . ," but to do *what,* to accomplish *what?* The uncertainty of the future beckons *and* alarms.

There is another disturbing aspect of this freedom, this creative possibility. How far does it extend? Are there any limits? Perhaps there are no limits. Perhaps one may become not only the "god of this world" but, as the serpent says, "like *the* gods." Then, as the serpent points out, one would not only banish ignorance—but also death.

For Adam or Eve none of these considerations can have been consciously marked or delineated, for they were in a state of innocence. What could the threat of death have meant concretely to one who had no experience of it? Or what could the notions "good and evil" have meant to one who was innocent? Nevertheless Eve is obviously aware, dimly and inchoately, of a threat (you shall die) and a promise (you shall be like the gods). The anxiety here is brooding and vague, but it is both fascinating and threatening.

I am suggesting that one basic aspect of the creative thrust of life itself is a kind of anxiety. If we did not have this urge to do, to become, to have dominion, we would not feel the threat of the unknown future or the exhilarating but disturbing uncertainty about the limits of our creativity. If there were no longing, we would be spared at least this kind of anxiety. And if we were not *anxious, we would not be longing*—rather we would already have attained or have suppressed the longing. Anxiety is one of the engines of our creativity. It is that sweet and bitter, exhilarating and frightening discontent that strengthens our urge to go on and yet sees the dangers of the enterprise.

The Anxiety over Guilt

Another prominent aspect of religious experience in every age and culture is anxiety over guilt. For example, Judaism and Christianity have to do with a righteous God before whom man feels guilty. Man is a sinner, and this sin is "the sting of death," for man fears that he will be eternally condemned for his sin. The religious drive is somehow to get free of this burden and threat.

In the case of anxiety over guilt, therefore, we do not seem to find anything creative. On the contrary, here is almost pure threat, so frightening that man will go to any lengths to get rid of the anxiety. Freud believed that religion is a kind of social compulsion neurosis, whose mechanisms were calculated to allay the anxiety of guilt. No one can deny that he illumined much in the religious life by turning upon it the light of his understanding of the conflicts between the super-ego and the other aspects of man's psychic life.

Even in this guilt-ridden form of anxiety there is a creative element. By this I do not mean simply that a horrible threat may lead a person to creative action. On this there can be no dispute. If one is frightened enough of his father's anger, he may be led to practice the piano, do his lessons, amount to something in the world. If one is frightened of God and of being damned to hell, he may, quite genuinely, become a saint. But in such an understanding, creativity is *extrinsic* to the anxiety of guilt—caused by it, as it were. We also know, however, that the anxiety of guilt can give rise to the opposite of creativity. If it is severe enough or if the person has too little strength, such guilt-ridden anxiety may lead to ego-restriction or to other crippling symptoms, even to a catatonic retreat from reality.

As the anxiety of guilt is viewed in the Christian context, there is a creative element *intrinsic* to it. I should like to illustrate this with reference again to the Adamic myth. As we have seen, Adam is in a situation of freedom, which involves a tension between creativity and dread of the unknown. But presumably his situation is not only bearable but, in a sense, idyllic, so long as he trusts God. He (Adam) need not have a map of the future so long as he walks with One who does—and One who provides him with all that is needed.

As we know from the myth, Adam did not remain in this relationship of trust. It is easy to understand his so-called Fall in terms of his violation of a specific rule—not to eat the fruit of a certain tree. But the great theologians have not seen this as the fundamental aspect of the Fall. The fundamental thing is the temptation to self-sufficiency and the consequent separation from God.

Man has creativity, the possibility of dominion—but within limits, since he is after all a creature. This very creativity leads him to entertain the possibility that his powers are unlimited, that he can be "like the gods," knowing good and evil, having complete dominion even over death. The temptation is to overstep the bounds of finitude, to take the future into one's own hands.

There is a Promethean quality about this. There is also a negative aspect. That is, there is a certain fear of the unknown future and consequently a desire to do something to manage and tame it, a desire to arrange for one's own security. This means that Adam is not content to trust God and face an open and unknown future. He wants security—on his own terms. Therefore, as Kierkegaard puts it, he "grasps at finitude"; he seeks something within his own ken (knowledge, nation, power) to defend himself against the unknown.

Both the expansive and shrinking aspects are present, but the upshot is "grasping at finitude," seeking in "the tree of knowledge" of a self-sufficiency that replaces trust in God with its demand to face an open and unmastered future. This is what is meant by original sin—not a specific misdeed, but a rupture of the relationship of trust, a separation from God.

According to the myth, Adam and Eve immediately felt the anxiety of guilt and the fear of punishment. They sought to hide from God. Why should they feel guilt and anxiety? The easy answer is that they feared punishment. Similarly one might argue that all religious anxiety over guilt is explainable by fear of punishment. Now I have no doubt that this explains many cases or that it is present as an ingredient in most cases. But is it not also possible, even necessary, to see in this situation the anxious concern of love or longing? Let me put it another way: What is the greatest punishment to be feared? Is it not the very separation from the loved object? Does not something like anxiety over guilt arise in very young children long before they understand punishment (in the ordinary sense of that term), or does it not arise even in the case of loving and permissive parents? Freud (and others) have suggested that the greatest fear of the infant is separation from the mother. And in later life anxiety over guilt retains the substructure of the anxiety over separation. One is anxious over his guilt because it means to him that he *deserves* the disapproval and rejection of the loved one. Fear of separation implies the positive impulse of tenderness, love, longing *about* the loss of which one is anxious.

You may object that often, especially in the case of the very young, this is not true love; rather it is self-regarding and sustained only by the physical need of the help of the other. I don't know how this question could be settled empirically, but I should be suspicious of separating this early, "narcissistic love" too sharply from mature "object love." Surely the latter grows out of the former by some mysterious process. In any case, the tender impulse toward the other is there and provides the basis for the creativity of later life.

To summarize, one not only sins, separates himself from God, and tries to be self-sufficient, but one feels guilty and anxious about his sin. If one were not anxious about sin, one would not be aware of it as *sin*. It is in the state of anxiety that we are aware of what we have done and of the good that we have (so we fear) lost. The feeling of guilt implies a positive desire for this good. As positive desire, it is just as much the basis for the healing process, as it is (*qua* fear) the basis for hiding and covering up. Whether the anxiety of guilt leads to healing or not, the creative effort to reunite with the loved object or to use pathology (mechanisms of defense and symptom formation) depends upon the total strength of the personality—and very importantly upon external factors, one of which I wish to mention later.

The Anxiety of Desire

Not so universal but nevertheless widespread is the explicitly mystical aspect of religious experience. The *Leitmotiv* of the mystic way is the desire for union with God. This is not to be interpreted as "identification" with God. At least in Western mysticism, to which I limit myself, the prominence of the ordinary language of heterosexual love makes it plain that this desire for union is desire for a loved object.

Longing for union is basically a creative, expansive impulse, which as a rule spills over in "works of love" in the world. But the longing is an anxious longing.[9] Teresa of Avila explains in her work, *Interior Castle,* that the closer one approaches the divine majesty the keener is one's anxiety.[10] In this case the anxiety is *predominantly* positive; one is anxious *to* complete his pilgrimage and be united. John Bunyan reports the following incident which occurred as two of his pilgrims neared the celestial city:

By reason of the natural glory of the city and the reflection of the sunbeams upon it, Christian with desire fell sick. Hopeful also had a fit or two of the same disease. Wherefore they lay by it a while, crying out because of their pangs, "If you see my Beloved, tell him that I am sick of love." [11]

Yet at the same time, according to Teresa, there are present two less creative aspects of anxiety: Sorrow for one's sins grows more acute the more clearly one sees how much he owes God and how good God is; and anxiety lest, even at this advanced stage, one should miss his goal. Desire is creative; but so long as it is desire and not consummation, it is anxious.

Danger and Object

I believe that the picture of anxiety which emerges from these descriptions of religious experiences is similar to that which emerges from clinical observations, if we keep in mind the fundamental structure which is implied. To be sure, Freud and others spoke of anxiety as a "reaction to danger." [12] I have already admitted that the reaction may be so strong, the danger perceived so overwhelming that the anxiety is morbid—that is, leads to disorientation or unconstructive responses. I have tried to show in the examples of religious experience that desire for God (for the loved object) is the fundamental context without which the anxieties of creativity, guilt, and desire cannot be objectively and accurately described.

How are these apparently diverse considerations to be reconciled in a unified theory of anxiety? Many problems stand in the way of a final solution. But a tentative suggestion may be in order—namely that we explore more systematically the connection, noted by Freud in the text to which I referred earlier, between longing (or desire) and anxiety. As Freud saw in the case of Hans, "increased affection" was fundamental in the anxiety, even though it appeared to be a morbid, disteleological anxiety.

This same suggestion may help us to distinguish anxiety from fear. Fear is aroused by a direct threat to one's self. It is more nearly an animal response, connected with the instinct of self-preservation. Anxiety is a more social, human response affectively similar to fear but different in the context which surrounds it. In anxiety the context is longing for another, even though for the infant the "other" is narcissistically defined. This means, as Freud says in one place, that in anxiety, the danger situation is always psychically equivalent to the danger of separation from the loved object.[13]

In this way we can account for both the negative and the positive aspects of anxiety. It is a reaction to danger, and may be so powerful as to disrupt the life of the individual. But the danger is dreadful precisely because it is a threat to something very much desired. So long as anxiety manifests itself, the desire for the loved object is presupposed. Where this positive and in theory potentially creative reference is totally lacking, we find no anxiety but catatonic stupor or death.

The Nature of Man

I referred at the outset to certain philosophers and theologians who hold that anxiety is a mirror in which we may see the reflection of human nature. I should like to suggest briefly how my reading of anxiety as being fundamentally a phenomenon of creative desire might affect one's view of man. My illustrations have been chiefly from the realm of religious experience. So I cast my suggestions on the nature of man in terms of an ancient theological doctrine, the image of God. An understanding of the creative aspects of anxiety may help to bring about a more constructive approach to this theological issue.

All Christian theologians have taught that man is created in the image of God. They could hardly avoid saying this, since it is said in Gen. 1. But one might almost say that at this point the agreement ends. Roman Catholic theologians, with great logical force, have maintained that the image of God was not lost with man's Fall into sin. Since the "image" is of the essence of man's creation, if it were lost, man after the Fall would be a different species. In that case, it would be most unjust for later generations to suffer for the sin of Adam. Nor could "man" (as we know him historically) be saved; he would have to be changed back into a different species. You can see how the notion of the loss of the image of God would lead to a thorny nest of problems—only a few of which I have mentioned.

The Reformed theologians have insisted, also with great logical force, that the "image of God" was in effect lost with the Fall into sin. To be sure, they have tried to hedge against saying it was utterly lost. They have been clever in making distinctions. Thus they have said that the "substance" of the image remained, but that it was stripped of all "attributes." Sometimes they have said that it remained but was totally ineffectual. They have said that if the image remained in any vital sense, man would tend to seek God. And if man tends to seek God, if there is any health in him, why was the terrible sacrifice of Christ necessary? Only the notion of the radical corruption of the image of God makes it possible to take sin seriously enough. Luther puts this in the following way:

> The scholastic statement that "the natural powers are unimpaired" is a horrible blasphemy. . . . If the natural powers are unimpaired, what need is there of Christ? If by nature man has good will; if he has true understanding to which, as they say, the will can naturally conform itself; what is it, then, that was lost in Paradise through sin and that had to be restored through the Son of God alone? [14]

These dilemmas can be mitigated, I believe, if we take a dynamic rather than static and substantive view of the image of God. Let us think of it not as an entity or substance which may or may not be lost. Let us think of it as a capacity to love, after the image and likeness of God's love. And, taught by dynamic psychology, let us understand that this capacity is not planted full-blown in the heart of the child; but that he has it, in a very real sense, as the end-point toward which his nature strives. This is the story, the destiny of every man (Adam).

What is the story of man? What is the status of this "image of God" which is his destiny, by virtue of the way in which he is created? It is the story of the perils *and* the possibilities of love; of the creativity *and* the fears of beings to whom fulfillment in love is the highest blessing, and separation from love the greatest punishment.

It is my contention that *anxiety is the child of love* and that in anxiety we can see the struggles of a free being moving toward or away from his destiny. But so long as anxiety is alive, it testifies to the struggle, to the fact that love may be beleaguered but is not lost. We all know, and we know more clearly as a result of the clinical work of psychiatrists, that the course of love does not run smoothly. There are the days of innocence and ignorance when the urge of love runs strong, but the fear of the unknown also looms. Then one is tempted to grasp at finiteness, to stop the developmental growth at some particular point where there seemed to be security. "I will be content with this little bit, rather than to try something new which might not be approved." There are the days of self-reproach, when one feels unworthy of the love of others. Then one is tempted to devise a rite of purification or to stop trying, so that one can't be blamed for his unworthiness (or any one of a thousand other strategies to allay the pangs of guilt). And even in our relative maturity, when we have found the loved one who returns our love, we are beset by fears that we are not worthy or that we may lose our beloved.

The changes that we are called upon to take a creative part in bringing about, so that we may at last realize the image of God, are fearful to finite and fragile beings. All of us at one time or another compromise our destiny. The anxiety that we experience not only tempts us to the compromise; it comes back upon us after the compromise, in a different form, to prove that our longing to become what we were meant to be is not dead. This anxiety of guilt, so long as we do not still it by narcotics or overly-severe self-limitations, drives us to seek a cure, drives us to resume our quest for the image of God.

One final point: The Reformed theologians were fearful of admitting that the image of God retained any vitality in fallen man, for they feared that this would suggest that man could achieve his destiny without the sacrificial love of Christ. But if we think of the image after the analogy I have suggested, we can admit its vitality and still understand quite clearly the need for help from beyond our own powers.

I have said that the course of love does not run smoothly. Who would deny that in every human being progress towards mature love (that love which freely gives to the beloved) is blocked in many ways, though with varying degrees of severity? When blockage does occur, help is needed; and the help that is needed is understanding, forgiving, accepting love. Psychoanalysis is predicated upon the fact that in some cases the blockages are so severe and begin to occur so early that specially trained people are needed to help the individual face his difficulty. But the special training would be of no avail without understanding and accepting the person in need.

The one who suffers needs to feel this love and acceptance. He cannot give it to himself—for this is just his problem: that he feels unworthy and therefore accuses himself. He must experience this love from another.

And now we must use an old theological word: The sufferer experiences this love as "grace"—as a gift freely given though undeserved. Only then, only after grace has opened the way, can the sufferer begin to realize the truth: that if this other one loves me, there must be something about me that *is* worthy after all. Anxiety is dreadful, but it is a sign of life. It accompanies us on our life's journey. And though we may be tempted to flee from it, it has a way of returning to haunt us, to remind us that no compromise with our fundamental destiny can give us rest, that only in the realization of the Divine Image, which is the Divine Love, can we find true or lasting fulfillment, can we find that love which casts out fear.

My comments might be taken as one man's elaboration of that famous prayer of Augustine: "Thou hast made us for Thyself and our hearts are restless till they rest in Thee." [15]

References

1. Martin Heidegger, *Sein und Zeit* (Halle a. d. S.: Max Niemeyer Verlag, 1935).
2. Sigmund Freud, "Inhibitions, Symptoms and Anxiety," *Standard Edition of the Complete Psychological Works of Sigmund Freud,* general ed. and trans. James Strachey (24 vols.; New York: The Macmillan Co., 1961). Used by permission of The Hogarth Press and Basic Books, Inc. XX, 82-174.
3. Sören Kierkegaard, *The Concept of Dread,* trans. Walter Lowrie (Princeton: Princeton University Press, 1944.) Used by permission.
4. Freud, *The Problem of Anxiety,* trans. H. A. Bunker (New York: W. W. Norton and Company, 1936). This was the title given to the first American edition. This work is identical with "Inhibitions, Symptoms and Anxiety," see note 2 above.

5. Freud, "Analysis of a Phobia in a Five-Year-Old Boy," *Standard Edition*, X, 5-149.
6. Freud, "Inhibitions, Symptoms and Anxiety," *Standard Edition*, XX, 144.
7. Kierkegaard, *The Concept of Dread*.
8. By the term "myth" I do not intend to suggest either that the story is untrue or that it is true in some special esoteric way. A myth is simply a story using symbols from everyday life to give an understanding of (alleged) events or realities at least some of which transcend ordinary experience.
9. Fred A. Berthold, Jr., *The Fear of God; The Role of Anxiety in Contemporary Thought* (New York: Harper & Row, Publishers, 1959).
10. St. Teresa of Avila, *The Complete Works of Teresa of Jesus,* ed. and trans. E. Allison Peers (3 vols.; New York: Sheed and Ward, 1946), Vol. II.
11. John Bunyan, *Pilgrim's Progress* (London: J. M. Dent & Sons Ltd., 1904).
12. Freud, "Inhibitions, Symptoms and Anxiety," *Standard Edition*, XX, 134.
13. *Ibid.,* p. 136.
14. Martin Luther, "Selected Psalms," *Luther's Works,* ed. Jaroslav Pelikan (St. Louis: Concordia Publishing House, 1955), Vol. XII.
15. Augustine, *Confessions,* trans. F. J. Sheed (New York: Sheed and Ward, 1943), p. 3.

You provide man with the stimulus that makes him want to praise you, because you have made us to be related to you and our inner existence is out of balance until it recovers its balance in right relation with you.

And we need not fear that we shall find no place to return to because we fell away from it. For, in our absence, our home—which is Thy eternity—does not fall away.

—PARAPHRASE OF AUGUSTINE

CHAPTER V

Anxiety and Grace: An Augustinian Perspective

Albert C. Outler

Some years ago Dr. Stanley Leavy and I were traveling together from New Haven to Washington, to *another* conference of psychiatrists and theologians. As our train flashed by Menlo Park, the Edison Memorial loomed on the right—as obvious a phallus as you might care to see. I pointed it out wordlessly. Doctor Leavy looked and nodded. "Yes, I know," he said dryly. "There are so many symbols and so few things to symbolize."

Mutatis mutandis, something of this sort can be said about the phenomena of anxiety. Almost anything may serve as an anxiety-generating symbol, but the symptoms of anxiety (that is, its physiological and psychological *affects*) are comparatively few and typically patterned. One can understand Freud's derivation of the root meaning of anxiety, *Angst,* from the Latin *angustiae,* since he normally uses it to refer to anxiety-*affects* (for example, cardiovascular acceleration, "chest tightening," inhibition of parasympathetic activity, and so on) . One of the original meanings of *angustia* is "a narrow passage" or "a dangerous strait"—and one of its obvious transferred meanings is: "being in a tight spot!" But if you wish to talk about the symbols of anxiety rather than its symptoms then the Latin word *anxius* is clearly closer to the mark —and is the actual prototype of our English word "anxious."

There seems to me to be a frequent and easy confusion in the literature I have read between the *anxii* (the signs of danger) and the alarm syndrome itself *(angustiae)* . This makes for real ambiguity in a discussion of the "constructive" uses of anxiety. You run straight into the unsteady distinction between anxiety as *cognition* (that is, signal-reading, recognition, and so on) and anxiety as *emotion* (that is, anxiety-affects). Thus one may hear it said that "anxious" people are more keenly aware of their environment because they are more sensitive to certain danger signals. This sort of heightened awareness *may* be, in some instances, "constructive." Or one may hear it said that anything which causes acute pain and disability is "destructive" and, obviously, the generality of anxiety-affects are painful and disabling. It might help, therefore, if we keep in mind that the "constructive" aspects of anxiety, to which I wish to point, have to do with anxiety as cognition.

It seems generally agreed that anxiety as affect is a mode of *primary attention.* Acute feelings of anxiety cannot be successfully ignored. They arise in a welter of apprehensions—real and imagined—and they range the spectrum from mild uneasiness to nameless horror. Yet there is a common motif throughout. This is *the fear of loss*—actual loss, imagined loss, and especially *impending loss.* Anxiety is not itself an appetition. Instead it is the dark shadow which accompanies appetition, as the dread of having our desires frustrated. Anxiety-affects register the fear that our felt needs will not be met or that we shall be deprived of something we cherish. Anxiety is the uneasiness in the face of a prospect of denial, rejection, miscarriage. The more significant our longings and aspirations, the more poignant—and "destructive" —are our anxiety feelings.

This general view, I have supposed, is in basic agreement with Freud's later doctrine of anxiety as our reactions to the perceived danger of nongratification, deprivation of love, protection, or fulfillment. Freud's analysis of the "sources" of anxiety seems to me straightforward and satisfactory, as far as it goes.[1] But it leaves open or begs the question as to whether there is such a thing as "ontological anxiety"—what some of you call "existential anxiety," or what Paul Tillich refers to as "fear of possible nonbeing." If there is such an *anxietas,* its *angustiae* would not differ markedly from any other alarm syndrome. But its reference would be different from the typical alarm symptom because of its greater generality and "ultimacy." Ontological anxiety is present when typical *anxii* do more than exacerbate our fear of loss and deprivation—when we are put in mind of our precarious existence and the prospects of transience and oblivion for ourselves and our values.

Heidegger grossly exaggerates the matter with his contention that the bulk of human anxieties serve their victims as mirrors of existence. At the very least, anxiety symptoms do not transmit their messages about the true import of life in any clear or self-evident form. All too much of what is alleged to be "existential" or "religious" anxiety is actually neurotic or "moral" anxiety (in Freud's specific use of that word). This is plain enough in the case histories of the existentialists themselves. Still and all, the anxiety is multidimensional—neurotic dread of loss may also be accompanied by and correlated with ontological dread of the degradation of being. There is a good deal of evidence that this is so—and if it is, we have an intelligible basis for construing ontological anxiety as potentially "constructive."

The theologian *as theologian* has a legitimate and competent interest in the constructive aspects of anxiety if, and only if, there is something like this ontological reference in our anxiety symptoms which is not essentially neurotic. Given some such premise as this, however, he may, with something close to propriety, suggest that anxiety (both as *anxietas* and *angustia*) provides men with clues to self-understanding and insights into their relationships with the Encompassing Mystery which constitutes our ultimate environment. Such clues and prods do not generate cognition by themselves. Actually they often give rise to fantastic and superstitious reactions. There is a positive correlation between anxiety feelings and the sort of magical thinking that Charles Odier has so skilfully analyzed. It is morally indefensible to speak of pain itself as "constructive." But if, in the strictures and suffering of anxiety, it happens that a man acknowledges the point of meeting between his existence and its ultimate ground, that act of acknowledgment *is* constructive. Thus if, even indirectly, anxiety symptoms prompt men to a valid cognition of the ultimate issues of life, they are highly significant and, at least in that sense, "constructive."

If something like this be the case, then it is the joint responsibility of psychiatrists and theologians to investigate the clues and prods of anxiety, to trace out their references both to the organic and ontological dimensions of human existence, and to make some educated guesses about the optimum conditions for human self-awareness and creativity. Psychiatrists have special skills in sifting out and rearranging the tangle of interpersonal communication involved in the disproportion between the *signs* of psychic danger and the *affects* of psychic dread. Theologians may be supposed to have had useful experience in reading the cracked mirror of existence into which men peer for reflections of their identities and destinies. Together these two perspectives on experience have much to offer each other and suffering mankind.

I take it as a commonplace that the first great Christian theologian to probe the inner life of man in search for clues to the truth about God and the world was Augustine of Hippo (A.D. 354-430). Here, as Windelband said, was "a metaphysics developed from the data of inner experience." There cannot be many of us unfamiliar with Augustine's best-known text: *Tu excitas ut laudare te delectet, quia fecisti nos ad te, et inquietum est cor nostrum donec requiescat in te*—and the familiar mistranslation of it: "Thou movest man to praise Thee, for Thou hast made us for Thyself and our hearts are restless until they rest in Thee." [2] It may be a minor matter about the mistranslation. The point is that here is a terse summary of a total perspective on human existence, which includes a specific message concerning the constructive uses of anxiety.

Cor nostrum is singular and means "our human heart," in the Biblical connotation of "heart"—as in "out of [the heart] are the issues of life" (Prov. 4:23). It could be rendered, quite accurately, as "the human condition"—man's situation in existence. *Inquietam* literally means "noisy," but by transfer it means a raucous clamor in "our heart." *Ad te,* again literally, means "in relation to you"—with the stress on communion rather than possession. *In te* means "in your presence," and does not involve the idea of "inclusion" or "absorption." We could come fairly close to the meaning of this text—which is as much as one may hope for in translating Augustine—with the following paraphrase: You (God) provide man with the stimulus that makes him want to praise you, but you have so fixed the human condition that it is disturbed until it returns to its "right relation" in your presence. This idea is one of the distinctive Augustinian motifs, repeated three times more in the *Confessions* and echoed everywhere else in his writings.

For Augustine, the most vivid anxiety symbol was disequilibrium in its various forms. It is almost as if he had converted his infantile fear of falling (or being upset) into a metaphor referring to man's groundlessness in existence. When a man has turned away from his right relationship to Being (*ad Deum*) he has lost his footing in Being (*in Deum*). Life is a scramble along a slippery path that skirts the cliff's edge. When we try to make our way alone or in the company of others no less fearful, we are actually ignoring or turning away from the real basis of our security—that is, *requiescans in Deum.* Our fears of falling arouse anxiety, whether they are justified or not. Anxiety, in its turn, prompts its victim to self-rescue by "magical thought" or anything else that offers. But this is the broad way to idolatry (*idolatria*) which means, in essence, putting your ultimate reliance on *any* creature or creaturely action.

Religious anxiety is both neurotic and ontological at one and the same time. It is neurotic to the extent that it misconstrues the symbols of "groundlessness" and so reacts *in*appropriately. From this follows the kaleidoscope of religiosity—with its superstitions and stultifying effects that the psychiatrist knows all too well. At the same time, our sense of alienation from God turns into a dread of God's alienation from us. The Deity is, quite literally, dreadful, and the guilt-ridden soul is anxious lest the offended Creator will jerk the rug out from under the offending creature, leaving him suspended over nothing! Augustine speaks of his dread of *abyssus*. The literal meaning of this term is "ocean-depths." Augustine had an anxiety-affect about the ocean: It reminded him—as neurotic anxiety feelings may remind anyone —of life's unsteadiness. Neurotic or no, the symbols of disequilibrium are reminders of the profoundest threat we ever recognize—life's lapsing into meaninglessness.

References to man's tragic insecurity are almost everywhere in Augustine's writings, but I have chosen to present a selection of samples in place of an exhaustive parade.[3] A companion metaphor to *abyssus* is the phrase "bottomless pit." Speaking of the storms of adolescence, he says: "I was tossed to and fro, wasted and poured out, and I boiled over." [4] In his nine years among the Manichees, he says, God "allowed [him] to tumble and toss around in the darkness—striving to rise but falling back again the more heavily." [5] The unrighteous stumble and fall; fleeing from God's goodness, they collide with his justice.[6] They stand vertiginous on a pinnacle shouting defiance at the heavens and then fall back again.[7] Anxiety gnaws at the soul which is unable to find equilibrium in any intellectual or practical certitude.[8]

In an interesting report of his "Plotinian ecstasy" Augustine tells how he experienced an acute sense of groundlessness,[9] and toppled back into the pit of uncertainty. His famous "conversion" in the garden at Milan was preceded by a vivid agitation. "I was greatly disturbed in the spirit, and angry with myself with a turbulent indignation . . . staggering and swaying about this way and that—a changeable, twisting, fluctuating will, wrestling with itself while one part falls as another rises." [10] At the climactic moment, he recalls, "I blushed violently . . . and hung suspended . . . This struggle raging in my heart was nothing but the contest of self against self." [11]

One of the most remarkable effects of his conversion and subsequent career was a marked reduction of anxiety symptoms. Life's pathway becomes firmer and clearer before him. Even in times of stress, his newfound *quietus* prevented his "toppling back into *abyssus*." [12] His life as a Christian was far from tranquil but the evidence is impressive that it was now poised in a buoyant medium which sustained him with a basic equilibrium. "God uplifts those cast down; they fall not for whom God is the most high." [13]

When Augustine tries to explain his own anxieties and others' he often speaks of *superbia*. This term, in its classical usage, means "haughtiness" or "arrogance"—but for Augustine it regularly denotes the pride that prompts such attitudes. It is the assertion of our will against God, a denial that our *quietus* can be found only "in God." "The primal *lapsus* of the rational creature . . . was the defection of his will . . . from the Good which is immutable." [14] When a man rests his weight upon the mutable goods of sight and sense, his "happiness" (*felicitas*) fluctuates with every change of circumstance. Anxiety is the inner dread of this unsteady support. Yet the truth is that there is no such thing as a firm footing in the created world itself. Those creaturely values on which we depend do not pretend to be a firm and final ground. Our feeling of groundlessness (and the dread of it) is meant to prod us toward the truth—that God alone is our true Ground and End.

Augustine was not a placid man nor a faultless one nor exempt from acute *angustiae*. His childhood was unhealthy; his adolescence neurotic. His mature life was spent in a demoralized world and he died in an uproar, with the Vandals battering at the walls of Hippo. His conscious longing was for "peace" but he found precious little of it in his outward circumstances.[15] Yet this same man—with his swollen id and raucous super-ego—lived and died with an inner steadiness and productivity, as if he had found his rest on bedrock, beneath life's heaving surfaces. He had found a "cure" for his ontological anxiety and this made all the difference in turning a gifted dilettante into one of the church's greatest "doctors."

The simplest form of Augustine's explanation of how anxiety may be fruitful runs something like this. God, the Ground of being even for those creatures who deny or defy him, has revealed *himself* as loving and sustaining, as able and willing to satisfy man's hunger for happiness, as active in human history and destiny. This *self*-manifestation of God's love, as it affects our hearts and lives, Augustine termed *gratia*. Without any close rival, this is the key word in the Augustinian vocabulary. It always connotes a divine action, for God's love is never inconsequential. Yet it is not a physical or palpable force. It works dynamic changes in human lives—there is a sense in which it is *irresistible*—but it is never impersonal and it does not abrogate human freedom. At least this is what Augustine says over and over again, and his disavowals should be seriously considered even by those who are unpersuaded by his arguments.

You will not demand an exhaustive word study of *gratia* and its cognates in the Augustinian corpus—and this is providential, since none exists and my own samplings are representative but not complete. God's grace is his active love toward men, which precedes and follows every human action; it is the primal and final ground of human capability.[16] *Gratia* prompts men to control and sublimate their irrational appetites (*cupiditas*) and thus promotes the highest level of health (*sanitas*). Grace buoys up the sinking spirit; it overmasters death's power to terrify us.[17] It enlightens our minds to know the good and energizes our wills "to do in love what we know in truth." [18] Nothing good begins without the initiative of grace; nothing is sustained or consummated without its continuance.[19]

In these and a multitude of other places Augustine makes plain that God's grace is God's therapy for man's *primal* anxiety. When it is recognized as *God's* grace and rightly acknowledged, it answers man's anxious longing for love and so changes what Dylan Thomas called "the weather of a man's heart." The quality or "feel" of our existence affects the way we perceive and value the events and relations in our experience. In an atmosphere of acute anxiety, a person will "decode" the anxiety signals that he perceives quite differently from one who feels upborne, accepted, beloved. Grace displaces one "atmosphere" (ontological anxiety) with another (ontological buoyance). Whatever their "destructive" effects, our anxieties may also confront us with the question about the quality of our existence: is it, at last and at bottom, hostile, neutral, or "gracious"? Every man *does* answer this question in every indication he makes of his ultimate concern.

The psychological sense of estrangement or "groundlessness" has an ontological implicate, whether this is consciously analyzed or not. Our fear of *abyssus,* our anxious longing for "quiet" can never be "quieted" by our own insouciance and courage. The weather systems of life are formed in the hinterland of "our heart" (*cor nostram*) where they march with the Encompassing Mystery of Being.

In the days of his rebellion and wayfaring, Augustine's heart's weather was notoriously unsettled. Every gain in insight served only to present fresh complications for his restless mind. Even when he had achieved a stable intellectual perspective (the neo-Plotinian idealism that he retained thereafter) his philosophical wisdom could not bring his libido under discipline. Looking back upon the vicissitudes of his pilgrimage, he realized that his constant difficulty had been his "aversion" from God and the consequent anxieties this brought on so that he might just go on sinking down into the self-obliterating void.

God's grace gave him a new grounding. He now felt himself established in being and truth, upborne by God's providence, sustained by his unwithdrawn love that is the very essence of Being. Grace means forgiveness of sins, the restoration of communion with God—with its demands and promises of "gracious living." It transvalued his self-understanding and sustained his courage in the midst of life's transience, in the face of death.

Does the action of God in grace override man's freedom? No, says Augustine, because our true freedom lies in the rational choice of the real possibilities of one's being; this choice is determined by what is real and not just what we prefer. The anxious man, rebellious or cowering, is "unfree" because of his unrealistic judgments about reality. These flow from his unstable footing in Being. It is important to notice that Augustine had already bypassed the conventional form of the problem of "freedom versus determinism" with his extraordinary notion of the different orders of time: past and future time on the one hand, and present time, on the other. The first two comprise the processes of recollection (*memoria*) and prediction (*exspectatio*). *Present* time, however, is a variable "moment," which may be "distended" or shrunk. Augustine called this *contuitus* ("contuition"). Past events are now determined; future events are even now determinate. But the present "moment" does not fall within the order of clock time and is thus "outside" the causal order. It is experienced not as sequence but as spontaneity. God's grace is irresistible in the sense that our hearts are made to respond to love: "We catch the spark of love from one who loves us." [20] When man recognizes and responds to God's grace—and this always happens in a living "moment"—his appropriate feeling is one of gratitude. Grace does not, therefore, usurp the will or act as a determinate cause in past and future times. What it does is to "fill" the *present moment* and thus affect the weather of the heart. Such gracious "moments" flow into *memoria* or look ahead, in *exspectatio*. *Memoria* is our sense of history. *Exspectatio* is our sense of the future.

The parallels and applications of this idea of causality in one sort of "time" and freedom in another would be well worth tracing out in contemporary psychotherapy. It is, to be sure, a dangerous doctrine and easily abused, as the history of Augustinianism plainly shows. Indeed in the bitter struggles with the Pelagians, Augustine so abused his own doctrine that the same church that denominated him its *Doctor Gratiae* quietly but firmly disengaged itself from his extreme views on irresistible grace and germinal predestination. Elsewhere I have tried to explain the contrast between Augustine's polemical and pastoral writings.[21] It is in these latter, where he is talking "within faith," that we find the authentic Augustinian perspective on anxiety and grace.

Those of us who share the catholic rejection of the Augustinian extremes are often baffled to hear them praised (as their proponets do regularly) as "comfortable doctrines"—in the literal sense of *confortare*—since their main concern is with the meaning of grace for the elect, whereas our anxiety about double predestination usually relates to its implications for the damned. If you regard predestination as a speculative chart of God's consignment of his human freight to their respective destinations, it is a monstrous and destructive doctrine. If you understand it as a rigorous insistence upon the prevenience of God's action to any human response—"who by thy love hath made us, who in thy love doth sustain us and who in thy love wouldst make us perfect"—you can recognize the truth for which Augustine, Pascal, and Barth have contended in their various ways.

I am not trying to exhaust the Augustinian viewpoint or to "settle" the question of anxiety and grace. There may be some who doubt that I have substantiated this mildly unconventional interpretation of Augustine. Others may be so indifferent to *this* particular angle of vision that it is all one to them whether my reading is right or wrong. More evidence might convince the critics; more grace might persuade the hostile. But if the broad lines of this perspective were accepted as valid, there would then follow some interesting implications for our current reflections upon anxiety.

We could begin by "defining" anxiety as a general reactive affect to a broad spectrum of *existentalia*, characterized by a dread of loss or deprivation of cherished values—a fear of groundlessness. The symptoms of anxiety (*angustiae*) are relatively standardized, but the anxiety-stimuli (*anxii*) are manifold beyond the organizing power of any psychological taxonomy. As I understand it, it is the psychiatrist's business to bring reason and love to bear upon the relations between stimuli and affect and to aid the destructively anxious person to a higher level of rational wisdom and responsible freedom. But if the reduction of anxiety-affects is the practical goal of therapy, its success can be a mixed blessing. Not all the dimensions of anxiety-tension can be reckoned as disabilities in human culture and interpersonal relations. There are strong anxiety-affects involved in all esthetic creativity and in every intellectual enterprise. I, for one, am impressed with how little we know about the inner dynamics of psychic tension and the *creative* uses of the imagination and inquiry. Part of our general anxiety about the current malaise of Western culture is some-how related to the reduction of certain age-old anxieties and the excitation of new ones unrelated to our basic grounding in nature. As ontological anxiety is "tranquilized" or alternatively "stylized," creativity falls stagnant.

And yet, of course, the vast flood of anxiety in the modern world is pitifully nonproductive. Nothing need be said in its approval or extenuation. It is easy to see an immense, palpating misery in modern life that must be reduced by all appropriate means, and the theologian must trust the psychiatrist to know better than other men what appropriate and feasible means there may be. But the theologian has some grounds for anxiety lest the psychiatrist try to reduce the cognitive-effects of anxiety in his rightful concern to reduce the destructive affects of it. There is evidence that modern psychiatry has not been altogether unprejudiced on this point.

It is quite true—and we theologians ought to have faced it more honestly—that religion furnishes many an appalling exhibit of neurotic anxiety, of which some of the saints and heroes of the faith are prime examples. There is a distressful lot of religiosity which has to be diagnosed as anxiety feelings converted into magic or phantasy. And yet it is also true that anxiety serves the function of posing the problem of selfhood in its ultimate dimensions. To get this done, whatever the circumstances and outcome, is thus far "constructive." Dread may not drive a man to faith. If temporary panic seems to do so, returning tranquillity will dissolve his "fixation." But the anxious man may be nearer to the point of asking the right questions about existence than the rigid-normal one—and also of hearing the right answers! If his anxious questions are ignored or psychologized (which amounts to the same thing in this context) the reduction of misery will not be accompanied by an equal increase in poise or competence. I would not wish to "pronounce" on the question as to whether "ultimate concerns" are legitimate items for consideration in the psychiatric interview save to make the obvious comment that *any* response to an expression of ultimate concern has ultimate implications, and "no answer" is still an answer.

Anxiety is not a "good thing" to be cultivated or celebrated. But if, as I have tried to suggest, there is such a thing as ontological anxiety, then grace is its "cure." Anxiety is the perversion of our longing for "the love which casts out fear." It is the dread that we shall lose or never have such love. It is the fear of being naughted, the horror of "groundlessness." Grace, on the other hand, is the love that steadies the soul, that upbears and sustains it as its Ground and End. It is at the end of his most important comment on death that Paul of Tarsus (himself something of an anxiety neurotic!) comes up with one of the steadiest words in the New Testament: "Therefore, my beloved brethren, be steadfast, immovable, always abounding in the work of the Lord, knowing that, in the Lord, your labor is not in vain" (1 Cor. 15:58 R.S.V.).

What if it actually were the case that we human folk are created *ad Deum?* What if one of the reasons our human condition (*cor nostrum*) is disquieted and distraught is that its only proper *quietus* is a *requiescans in Deum?* What would follow if it were true that the quality of our courage for life and death depends, at bottom, on the relation we bear to the Encompassing Mystery of Being—whether we regard that Mystery as neutral, hostile, or gracious? We then would have a theological accounting for the restlessness and rootlessness of the human spirit, an explanation for the uneasiness which every sensitive man feels within himself or in any "standing order." It would shed light on the profoundly important images of "the pilgrim" and "the pioneer" in those societies that have a sense of linear time. It would be more than a marginal note to the thrust of history beyond itself—the claim of life to a meaning more than happenstance.

It would describe the sort of serenity that "our heart" requires: a *quietus* in which being loved and loving are the main determinants of our psychic atmospheres; a *quietus* which is not a terminus or even a status, but rather the gyroscope that helps hold the prow of life head-on into the breaking waves of the future. Finally, this view would explicate the notion that God's grace is not a flaw in his sovereignty but its most impressive verification:

For our stability, when it is in Thee, is stability indeed; but when it is in ourselves, then it is all unstable. Our good lives forever with Thee, and when we turn from Thee with aversion, we fall into our own perversion. Let us now, O Lord, return that we be not overturned, because with Thee our good lives without blemish—for our good is Thee Thyself—and we need not fear that we shall find no place to return to because we fell away from it. For, in our absence, our home —which is Thy eternity—does not fall away.[22]

References

1. Cf. Calvin Springer Hall and Gardner Lindzey, "Psychoanalytic Theory and Its Applications in the Social Sciences," *Handbook of Social Psychology*, ed. G. Lindzey (2 vols.; Reading, Mass.: Addison-Wesley Publishing Company, Inc., 1954) , I, 160-65.

2. Augustine, *Confessions*, ed. Pierre de Labriolle (Paris: Les Belles Lettres, 1950) , p. 31.

3. From *Augustine: Confessions and Enchiridion*, ed. and trans. Albert C. Outler. Vol. VII, LCC. Published 1955, The Westminster Press. Used by permission.

4. Augustine, *Confessions, op. cit.,* p. 50.

5. *Ibid.,* p. 75.

6. *Ibid.,* p. 96.

7. *Ibid.,* p. 87.

8. *Ibid.,* p. 117.

9. *Ibid.,* p. 146.

10. *Ibid.,* p. 170.

11. *Ibid.,* p. 175.

12. *Ibid.,* p. 179.

13. *Ibid.,* p. 269.

14. *Ibid.,* p. 353.

15. Cf. Albert C. Outler, "Augustine and the Transvaluation of the Classical Tradition," *The Classical Journal*, December 1957, LIII, 3.

16. *Augustine: Confessions and Enchiridion* and "On Nature and Grace," "On the Grace of Christ," *Basic Writings of St. Augustine*, ed. W. J. Oates (New York: Random House, 1948) , Vol. I.

17. *Augustine: Confessions and Enchiridion* and Augustine, *The City of God* (New York: Modern Library, 1950) .

18. Augustine, "On Rebuke and Grace," *Nicene and Post-Nicene Fathers*, ed. Philip Schaff (New York: Christian Literature, 1887) , Series I, Vol. V.

19. "Against Two Letters of Pelagius," *ibid.*

20. *Augustine: Confessions and Enchiridion*, p. 88.

21. *A Companion to the Study of St. Augustine*, ed. R. W. Battenhouse (New York: Oxford University Press, 1955) , p. 360-63.

22. *Augustine: Confessions and Enchiridion*, p. 94.

"Every human love is the love of God unaware of itself."

—ETIENNE GILSON

"I don't know why but I guess I'm really afraid if I expose myself to God that I never could recover if anything happened."

—A CLIENT IN COUNSELING

CHAPTER VI

Positive Anxiety in Judaeo-Christian Thought

Charles A. Curran

As I understand the topic, "Positive Anxiety (or Constructive Anxiety) in Judaeo-Christian Thought," it is intended to mean the basic components that seem to enter into anxiety in the positive sense as it shows itself in the whole Judaeo-Christian tradition and not simply in what might be called Catholic writings. In this sense I see my topic as "Catholic" in the whole Judaeo-Christian sense. But this would also be the basically Catholic tradition too.

Obviously, so conceived, this is an extremely broad and inclusive kind of topic. I propose to confine myself to a more limited treatment and, in the light not only of my philosophical and theological interests but also of my clinical interests as well, to consider somewhat the clinical implications and aspects of anxiety in the Judaeo-Christian tradition, as well as its more philosophical and theological components.

Consequently I would like to single out two main and continually recurring impulses or—to use a presently popular word—two *main* "thrusts" (I emphasize the word "main," there are many other such thrusts) that the Judaeo-Christian tradition introduces into the question of positive anxiety. The *first* of these is the movement toward maturity: the "anxious striving" to be a mature and responsible religious person as well as a psychologically and physically mature person. The *second* is a profound sense of the transiency of all immediate, earthly goals, but not their rejection—and consequently an "anxious longing" for lasting security, fulfillment, and ultimate being and becoming in an increasing participation in the person and being of God. We might therefore summarize these two thrusts as an "anxious striving" to total maturity and an "anxious longing" for finally being oneself in Ultimate Being in a pantheistic sense.

Anxious Striving

The English essayist, G. K. Chesterton, once described a young man who left England on a journey of discovery. He was determined to discover by himself a perfect country and there settle and raise a family. He went from city to city, from civilization to civilization, from the most primitive to the most developed in a difficult and thorough search. Finally across a sea he came to an unknown shore and found there if not a perfect setting at least one that was the most satisfying. And as he explored in delight his newly found land, he climbed a hill to look at a new landscape and there saw off in a distance the gleaming towers of the cathedrals and buildings of London. He had found by long and arduous pursuit what he had, in a way, always known and loved.[1]

The growth of a person toward maturity is, as I have seen it, an anxious striving for values and personal meanings but not in the usual sense of these phrases. Whether he does this through a counseling or psychotherapeutic or some intense learning relationship, his "anxious striving" results rather in an adventurous, thrilling personal pursuit in an independent and sometimes seemingly dangerous way of values which are uniquely new and are his own. Moreover as this process moves forward, one of the most consistent things I have observed is the increasing anxiety of the person, particularly the younger person, to safeguard his newly acquired cache of self-determined values and to resist forcibly anyone trying to impose values from the outside without these values being genuinely assimilated by him.

But for me the surprising thing here is, as Chesterton's analogy suggests, that this intense and independent pursuit and anxious striving does not necessarily produce social rebellion or philosophical and theological anarchy. Rather the opposite seems most often to happen. When the person with deep personal integrity and security probes himself, he finds, sometimes to his surprise in this absolutely personal pursuit, many of the basic values that are most fundamental to our whole Western secular and religious civilization, values which in varying forms are held by all civilized societies if these societies are really understood. Here it seems to me with a strange twist and in a way G. Stanley Hall and others of his time would perhaps never have dreamed, we see that "ontogeny recapitulates phylogeny."

At the same time, in proportion as this person is religious, he applies this same anxious concern to rethinking of his whole relationship with God. In this rethinking process he sees his relationship with God as more mature, responsible, honest, independent, and really "loving" in place of an artificial and protective fear of God or a childishly immature and often somewhat irresponsible dependency.

Although he may often not realize it, in this the person is, in fact, demonstrating the very deepest concepts of Judaeo-Christian mature and responsible religious growth. Here Paul's expression, "When I became a man, I put away the things of a child," (I Cor. 13:11 Douay), catches the core of this tradition. This in no way contradicts our becoming "as little children," as Christ directs. We can distinguish the childlikeness, the candor, the directness that is characteristic of a spiritually and psychologically mature person from the childishness of the infantile or pusillanimous person. There is, therefore, in the spiritual process the same anxious striving for religious maturity that one finds in the basic drives for other kinds of independent and responsible maturity. We are proposing here not something totally different, but rather the recognition of a religious dimension in the believer that is interrelated to and interwoven with these common, positive anxious concerns.

To demonstrate clinically what we mean here, let me cite an extended excerpt from a recorded counseling interview with a woman graduate student.

In this excerpt the young woman is in the midst of an intense and thorough personal reevaluation. In the previous interviews of this series she had unfolded and clarified for herself that while college and graduate work were satisfying achievements they still left her feeling that she had no value as a person. This was the same worthless feeling which she had had almost as long as she could remember. She was able to trace the origin of this to some of her earliest childhood experiences when, for a very short period only, she remembered herself as being accepted and loved. Then with the coming of a younger sister and a switch in family circumstances, she became definitely a burden, particularly to her mother. From here on, in her homelife, she could only remember veiled criticism and rejection coupled with adolescent antagonism from the younger sister because she was physically more attractive and more socially acceptable than her younger sister. The mother, too, seemed to foster this antagonism because she preferred the younger sister.

In this interview she has come finally to accept herself as a person of worth and meaning and she now finds that she must establish a whole new personal plan of life:

Client: But now as I no longer see myself as a failure—I mean, I basically feel that, that I'm worthwhile and, and that I can do well in a lot of things—seeing that on one side and no longer feeling worthless, I still have yet to see things in true perspective. I mean, I can see that the thing is not on this side of the card, but is on the other side of the card, but I still don't know exactly what's on that side.

As the excerpt continues, we notice that for this young woman the reacceptance of herself has many of the qualities of a new birth. Unfortunately the printed page cannot reproduce the gentle, hushed tones of her voice. It seemed to the counselor not unlike a woman's first wonderment at having a child. Throughout this excerpt she is speaking slowly, almost meditatively but with intense feeling. The interview continues:

Counselor: It's a new way of evaluating yourself, and therefore it needs a great deal more delineation.

Client: Uh-huh. This is the first time I've felt free to do that . . . and it's deep. I think I'm going to cry again. I mean it's like a, a new baby. You're afraid its skin or something is fragile. (*Sobbing softly, she pauses*) And forcing it to come out this way is the only way to do it.

Because there no longer remains any possibility of its being something unreal, because it's something recognized in reality that is actually taking place, like a project. Whereas if you just think about it, you'd never be sure and you really can never take anything, any growth, or anything positive from it.

Another thing, this is the one time when I have really got everything out that was in myself and when nobody did anything about it—like at home, you know, when I would have been criticized—I mean, it was just accepted. And I suppose that's why I have played so many roles and been so artificial, because I suppose in a way I was hurt very deeply at home. I was sort of determined that, well, if it happens once shame on you, but if it happens twice shame on me, and I wasn't going to be caught again I suppose. (*Pause*) Because, I mean—their statements and so on if they were objectively true, it would have been all right, but they weren't. You could have accepted it if it was a real situation, but when you realize that, that it was wrong, well then, you just don't want to take any chances on its happening again.

And I suppose that probably happens to a lot of people. And I don't suppose—if it hadn't been for this I know I would never have changed. I suppose it is very unusual for it to have broken and come out again.

In the next interview her reevaluation goes beyond her relationship to herself and others and penetrates through to her relationship with God:

Client: I was thinking—as a result of that last interview it was almost like a rebirth again. As I thought about it during the week I realized that the same thing I had felt before in relation to all other people, I felt also in relation to God. I don't think I really basically could feel a real wholesome relationship. I don't think I could feel that God could really love me. But as a result of that interview and now here, I really see that very clearly.

I can go along so long and pray and then all of a sudden I'm back again to the very beginning and I feel as though I've never had anything in a spiritual way. And I think that's the reason, because I just can't feel that it can be so *(Cries softly)*, that I could have value in God's eyes.

As the interview continues, she draws a parallel between the realism which the counselor represents to her and that same relationship with God:

Client: *(Pause)* And something like the way I can't look at you very well *(laughs)*, I can't look at God.

Maybe the connection is to what I said before that you were the first person that I couldn't fool. And in that way—because for so long I have lived in a world where I knew that I was all covered up, so to speak, sort of insulated from everyone for so long *(pause)* so there just aren't any experiences, you're just not able —I'm thinking of new skin or something again—when the skin has been burned you can't put it near real bright lights or something like that.

I don't know what that goes back to, I don't think I've had a tragic life or anything of that sort. I don't know why but I guess I'm really afraid if I expose myself to God that I never could recover if anything happened *(crying softly)*.

As the interview continues she explains that she was always aware how this artificiality, so characteristic of her relationship to everyone, was also affecting her relationship to God. Yet until she had cleared away all these other sources of worthlessness and defense she was not able to face herself with such a thorough and ultimate evaluation.

Client: This is awfully hard to talk about *(pause)*.

I've always felt that in relation to this. And I think that's maybe one reason why I never, why I would never actually face it before. Well, probably not the only reason because I did have other areas to work out *(pause)*. It's funny, in some ways I want to laugh but not because it's humorous or not because it's light. I don't know exactly why *(pause)*.

I guess I'm just glad to be able to face these things now. But,

I'm afraid to talk about them too—because they are so meaning-ful that I don't want any of that artificiality (*pause*), which I am so capable of, to spoil them (*She speaks very slowly, seeming-ly having difficulty controlling her voice*).

Yes, and the reason that is so is because I don't know where I started to be artificial (*pause*). But the reason that has meaning here is because being able to be that way, at school especially, with the Sisters (*pause*) when I was first beginning to learn about prayer and things like that (*pause*) I never could be sure that anything religious wasn't as artificial as I was. (*Sobbing, long pause*) And the thing is so awful because I think the things I did as a child were so right, I mean, it was true that was the right thing but it was because of all the deceptiveness and artificiality, I could have no certitude that it was true and then as I grew older (*pause*), as I wanted to throw that artificiality off, you see the thing to do was to throw off. Too, so much of what I saw was in a religious way artificial for me. I can see how people would easily give up their faith, would easily lose all the richness of it because of that. In my personal life there was truth and the purest truth and yet the worst deception wedded so closely together that I could never separate them (*pause*).

In these excerpts, we see how a person's constructive responsi-bility steadily develops as she grows encouraged "to be herself" in the best meaning of this phrase and finds acceptance and under-standing of that self in the unsparing realism of the counseling interview. Through this she can make a positive growth in in-creased "being" herself. This brings her not only to an honest and sincere facing of herself in the light of her own reasonable judg-ment but also to a confidence that others, knowing her as she really is, can accept and love her too. But most of all, God himself now becomes for the first time a real and loving Being and not a fear-some image from which she must hide in her artificiality. Here then is a respect for self which, previously side-tracked by con-fused and disordered life-reactions, now gives birth to an increas-ingly mature honesty, respect, and regard for others and a final facing of herself and God.

What we see here is a growth of self—the new birth of a mature person—a true being oneself. This is a growth away from artificiality and withdrawal. It is motivated by a positive anxiety to be honest with oneself, to face and accept responsibility for oneself, to become a genuinely mature person who is at the same time a religiously mature person. Both strivings for maturity are interwoven and unified.

Consequently in this first religious thrust of *anxious striving*, we are not changing the nature of man's struggle for maturity in all its psychosomatic components as Selye might describe them, nor in its id-ego-super-ego conflicts as Freud would see them. These issues still remain. The Judaeo-Christian tradition would simply add a further force and dimension.

This force and dimension is as strong and extensive as the person's faith in a Divine Being and his conviction of a particular religion as the voice of that Being. Put another way, intense and intelligent religious faith introduces another voice into the counseling or therapeutic dialogue and diagnosis because it introduces another—in this case, supernatural—Person into one's hope and love relationship. The intensity of a person's religious faith, his religious investment or commitment in other words, will determine how loudly or softly he hears this voice and how important its presence is to him. Assuming a strong religious faith, however, we have in this striving for a mature, religious self an often untapped source for growth. This does not change the person's struggle and conflict in gaining maturity but adds—in proportion to his religious faith—a concomitant weak or strong new positive force and dimension to all his positive anxious concerns.

In the light of this new positive force and dimension, which a strong, mature, and firm religious faith introduces, it might be interesting to explore briefly some parallel aspects in the religious man's positive relationship with God and similar aspects as they show themselves in the counseling relationship. Moreover what we say here of the counseling relationship could apply equally to all forms of psychotherapy as well as perhaps to many of the best kinds of educational relationships. Or put another way, wherever any form of man's positive "anxious striving" is seen, it has some of these same components.

The first parallel (we use the word parallel here so as not to confuse or equate the two relationships: man with man, man with God) with the religious experience is the commitment of self. In religious literature this is usually called "faith" or "love" or both. But the religious man must give himself to the divine relationship and believe and trust in God's love, understanding, and acceptance of him even at the deepest level of his own self-misery and inadequacy. The deepening counseling or therapeutic or learning process seems to produce a similar kind of trusting oneself to the relationship. As one client remarked to the counselor, after an interview, "You know, through this experience I can understand for the first time how God can really love me."

That is, a person, having communicated himself without reserve discovers that the counselor's understanding extends to all facets of himself, even to those he may have kept hidden from others and even from himself. This has helped him to his first real understanding of how God could love and accept him at the same profound level.

Here we note a second mutual term "communion." The religious person "communes" with God; the client and the counselor, the patient and therapist, the teacher and learner "communicate" together. Even though human communication is apparently limited to the dialogue, much more than words go into what is really exchanged. The communication between man and the Divine Being too can go beyond verbal prayers to an intense sense of belonging, of sharing and being understood, and understanding. Through the counseling dialogue, the client seeks to be understood and thus to understand himself. It is in a way the counselor's striving to understand him that intensifies the client's own efforts to understand himself and to communicate and share with the counselor what he slowly and sometimes tortuously is discovering about himself. As another client puts it, "Because you are trying so hard to understand me, I'm urged all the more to want to explain myself clearly to you and to myself."

We have, then, a third parallel: The religious man's conviction from his divine commitment that God's love and acceptance is both a deep understanding of him at the level of his weakness and at the same time produces in him an intense urge or what we have called a positive anxious striving to "better" himself. This is not accomplished merely by some process simply of "positive" thinking, but rather to "become" more really himself, to "be" himself as God made him. But this "being" and "becoming" oneself for the religious man implies a real possibility of realization and fulfillment that urges him on constructively. We have a movement here not only of faith but of hope.

So the client, patient, or learner too is thus urged to movement and growth, not because he is condemned or criticized, but rather because he knows he is understood and understands and somehow is freer to become and to be himself in a more completely integrated way.

This also has a religious parallel. To quote the New Testament again, It is "not as though we had loved God, but because he hath first loved us, and sent his Son to be a propitiation for our sins" (I John 4:10 Douay). The religious man, in faith, has the security that God respects, loves, and accepts him, and through this he can grope for self-respect, love, and acceptance of himself. At the very highest point here we have the theological concept of redemption and its fruits being extended to all men, depending only on their free and responsible cooperation. The conviction that no man is so alone or so unworthy that these effects cannot reach him is a profound and unanimous voice in the Judaeo-Christian tradition.

Anxious Longing

The second thrust in the personality coming from our Judaeo-Christian tradition we have called *positive* anxious longing.

In some of the old classic Dutch and Italian paintings, it was the artist's practice, as Stephen Tennant has pointed out, to give a

drawing-room or kitchen, in which there is a window open, through which you see the masts of ships, or a strip of grey sea . . . [or] vistas of colonnades or a balcony, a garden or a court. [The experience afforded the viewer here] is essentially one of gazing beyond the immediate scene to a timeless sky or a timeless room, in which the future and the past, the unspoken and the unknown, forever beckon.[2]

If we were to ask what this theological anxious longing introduces into the personality, we might answer that, like the Dutch and Italian paintings, it always suggests this "gazing beyond the immediate scene to a timeless sky or a timeless room" into vistas that extend to eternity. The religious man always questions from ultimate values, always looks to the room beyond, reminding himself with Paul that "here we have no lasting city."

In his discussion of dreams Freud remarks, "Anxiety is only fastened on to the idea that accompanies it and is really derived from another source." [3]

The Judaeo-Christian tradition would make this ultimate source of anxiety—whatever its more immediate sources might be—the intense desire to possess and to belong to a Divine Person who is Love itself. "God is love," John explains, "and he that dwelleth in love dwelleth in God, and God in him" (I John 4:16 Douay). The philosopher Gilson put it another way, "Every human love is the love of God unaware of itself." [4]

That is to say, as the sun permeates every nook and cranny of the earth with its light, so Divine Love, in the Judaeo-Christian tradition, permeates every human love and relationship. Stated again in the words of John: "He that loveth not his brother whom he seeth, how can he love God whom he seeth not?" (I John 4:20 Douay.)

If we put this in the Judaic analogy found in the Psalms, we have the religious man as the explorer, struggling through the complex underbrush or hot sands of daily living or finding his footing when he is mired down in muck on the rock that is God, as the psalmist says. (Ps. 94:22.) But in this tortuous journey he always can see in the distance, as the sixty-eighth psalm says, "the hill which God desireth to dwell in; yea, the Lord will dwell in . . . for ever." This divine awareness encourages and guides him so he is never wholly lost and yet offers him a final goal and destiny that gives meaning to his journey and its joys and sorrows. Or as in the Psalm that remains perhaps the most consoling and reassuring statement of the Judaeo-Christian faith, he has the Good Shepherd to lead him to green pastures.

Here too, however, as with the first thrust of *anxious striving*, the second thrust of *anxious longing* is not separated from all other longings of an immediate and pressing nature, as we might see them for example in psychotherapy. Rather these immediate and ultimate longings are intimately interwoven. There is no other worldly removal or withdrawal. In the mainstream of the Judaeo-Christian tradition—and here it differs with some of the Oriental religious traditions—the religious "anxious longing" is part of all the other positive anxious longings that make up the motivations of a man's strivings. As the sun permeates the earth and the traveler must go through the underbrush, muck, and sand to the mountain, so the religious longing permeates and is integrated with all other human goals and purposes.

But here we now come to some aspects that go beyond the counseling, psychotherapeutic, or learning relationship. At no point here do we wish to suggest that religion is a substitute for these or vice versa. Each of these relationships, while they may parallel one another in certain ways, is in fact essentially and basically different, and therefore one can in no way substitute for another. This becomes evident when we consider how religious values extend beyond. In fact when counseling, psychotherapy, or any form of healing fails or is increasingly inadequate, it is precisely here that religious values and factors have their most significant power and meaning.

Another way of saying this is that the Judaeo-Christian tradition suggests a third dimension in the psychosomatic relationship of the self and the other—this third dimension is the theological need in man. In a certain sense we might say that in detailing the religious aspect of psychological dynamics we are going beyond Freud to Augustine. Augustine agrees with Freud that at the deepest self-level one finds only restlessness, inadequacy, and sometimes even frightful disorder. Augustine concluded from this, and here he voiced the Judaeo-Christian tradition, that man has an intrinsic capacity, a yawning need that he himself cannot fulfill nor can others fulfill it for him. He is restless at the very core of his being for something infinitely beyond himself. Consequently for Augustine anxiety was inevitably behind every human goal or love. Behind every such achievement or value was the nagging fear of loss and resultant misery and emptiness. Only the possibility of achieving God and the infinite quest of knowing and loving God could give final meaning and security to all human goals and loves. These were, so to speak, reflections of divine goodness and love, the becomings which would fuse into an eternity of Divine Being—not a static state but an eternity of personal unfolding fulfillment in God. This, Augustine felt, was what man was really made for, and no other person, achievement, or value could satisfy and alleviate, except temporarily, his profound anxiety and restless inner quest. This quest and anxiety may be stilled for a time by such temporal meanings, but it comes back each time with even greater force when these temporal meanings are threatened with loss.

Consequently it is in this third theological dimension of positive anxious longing that religious factors and values add to all forces of healing or personal aid. This third dimension for the religious man goes beyond the somatic world of pain and the psychological world of conflict and fear to a divine commitment mutually shared between God and man. It is an "I-Thou" relationship with God where, in a relationship and dialogue with the Divine Being, man has confidence and security in an ultimate "being" and "becoming" in the most complete sense of self-unfolding and fulfillment at the highest level of his own personality. This being and becoming goes beyond death, in the Judaeo-Christian tradition. For while death ends the anxious striving and takes away all the immediate goals and values of such striving, it is not seen as a defeat or as a loss but as a victory and fulfillment. "O death, where is thy sting?" (I Cor. 15:55.) The triumphant cry of Paul can be a challenge hurled at death in the Judaeo-Christian tradition because death and the end of anxious striving

117

is but the portal to the positive religious fulfillment of all positive anxious longing. Anxiety comes full circle from striving and longing to fulfillment.

References

1. G. K. Chesterton, *Orthodoxy* (New York: Sheed and Ward, 1939).
2. Willa Cather, *On Writing*, "Foreword" by Stephen Tennant (New York: Alfred A. Knopf, Inc., 1949).
3. Sigmund Freud, "The Interpretation of Dreams." *Standard Edition of the Complete Psychological Works of Sigmund Freud,* general ed. and trans. James Strachey (24 vols., New York: The Macmillan Co., 1953). Used by permission of The Hogarth Press and Basic Books, Inc. Vols. IV, V.
4. Etienne Gilson, *passim.*

"Every concept must be dealt with as from that science to which it belongs, whether the concept belongs to the science in such a way that it is developed there or is developed by being presupposed."

—Sören Kierkegaard

CHAPTER VII

Anxiety: Affect or Cognitive State?

Paul W. Pruyser

When such affect-laden words as "fear," "anxiety," or "apprehension" become topics of scientific discourse and when, in debate or dialogue, attempts are made to distinguish among types of anxiety, it is obvious that the problem of definition is paramount. In the first place, such words purport to describe feelings, affects, moods, or sentiments whereas no task in psychology has proved more difficult than the description of emotional states. Artists and writers have given more penetrating and convincing portrayals of emotion than even the most elaborate psychological textbooks. In the second place, descriptions of emotion have also the capacity to arouse feelings in the reader or listener; one gets tuned in to the meanings and tends to experience empathically at least some fragment of their affective charge. Third, affect-describing words, even when toned down by the non-emotionality of science, tend to make us select referents from our own private world rather than the objective and common world we share with others. On hearing the word "anxiety" one is spontaneously prone to consider his own anxiety experiences as the best and most lively examples.

Our direct and private experiences with anxiety then suggest that proprietary attitudes toward our topic are to be expected. Anxiety is not likely ever to be discussed as objectively as, for instance, furniture, soil depletion, or the mating behavior of flatworms. It is to be expected that people in debate will contend about anxiety (that is, *their* anxiety) anxiously and engagingly, polemically, emotionally and thus very privately, with diminished regard for the success or failure of communication. While this may add a note of liveliness to debate, it inhibits the possibility of fruitful dialogue and mutual enrichment of understanding. Add to this the contention of some people that anxiety is disruptive while others contend with equal vehemence that anxiety is a prerequisite for growth and creativity, and it will be clear that sensible discourse about anxiety is not easy to achieve.

Problems in Defining Anxiety

From the very start, the problem of definition is augmented by the uncanny "inside-outside problem" or what some linguistic analysts would call the issue of consensual validation. This has been sharply put by Szasz who wrote:

In the case of the distinction between objective fear and neurotic anxiety, it is not the experience of anxiety that is being classified but rather its nature (or cause) according to the judgment of the observer. The observer is usually another person (another ego) although it may be simply another portion of the ego (that is one part of the ego observing another part). The problem is one of validation.[1]

A second serious obstacle to fruitful discussion is the failure to distinguish between what may be called "molar" and "molecular" conceptions of anxiety. To the molar conceptions I would assign the Stoic notion, nicely summarized by the Arab scholar, Ali ibn Hazm (994-1064): "No one is moved to act, or resolves to speak a single word, who does not hope by means of this action or word to release anxiety from his spirit." In this case, anxiety has become the sole explanatory concept for all behavior, with the result that one ends up in a hopeless syncretism. By contrast, Freud's first anxiety theory, the so-called toxicological theory, which considered anxiety to be the product of undischargeable libido quantities, is a rather molecular point of view. Even more molecular is the view of J. B. Watson in regard to fear which is emptied of its subjective content and pertains merely to a specific motor reaction in response to a specific extraneous stimulus situation.

While the adjectives "molar" and "molecular" adhere in this case to the concrete behavioral referents or the model-exemplar of the word *anxiety,* the *concept* of anxiety itself may also be broad or narrow. Some writers favor a narrow delineation of the concept and try to differentiate anxiety from fear, fright, terror, panic, despair, and so on, while others prefer a more generic concept of anxiety, with or without subtypes. To some, anxiety is nearly synonymous with tension-awareness and is thus linked with the idea of stress; to others, it has a specific phenomenology which points to an intrinsic quality or essence.

All these and several more differences will have to be kept in mind before one can proceed with even a simple, low-level analysis of the meanings of the term "anxiety" to different professional groups. Since the preceding papers represent basically two disciplines, the psychiatric-psychological and the existential-theological, I shall confine my analysis to these groups. As the analysis proceeds we shall find two major clusters of definitions: an emotional one which is maintained by most clinicians, and a cognitive one which is espoused by many theologians.

The division between these two groups should not be taken to imply homogeneity of opinion within each group; there is indeed ample room for individual differences. Neither should the division be stated as a categorical one, for interpenetration between the two viewpoints is possible and has been attempted.

Let us now look at the different contexts within which the term anxiety is considered a meaningful datum or concept for the two groups: first the clinical context, then the philosophico-theological context.

The Clinical Context

Our interest lies not in an exact reconstruction of the history of the clinical term "anxiety" and its cognates nor in establishing historical priorities in their use. Even the most cursory survey of the nineteenth century textbooks of psychiatry shows that the clinical significance of anxiety was not discovered in our age, but that the clinicians of the previous age were familiar with it, at least with some of its major forms. A retrospective look seems to indicate that it was left for our age, under the impact of psychoanalysis, to give anxiety a more central role in the etiology and phenomenology of mental disorder. But in doing so, psychoanalysis synthesized earlier observations which were less well integrated and understood.

In 1827, Benjamin Rush wrote:

> There are so much danger and evil in our world, that the passion of fear was implanted in our minds for the wise and benevolent purpose of defending us from them.
> The objects of fear are of two kinds.
> I. Reasonable. These are, death, and surgical operations. And,
> II. Unreasonable. These are, thunder, darkness, ghosts, speaking in public, sailing, riding, certain animals, particularly cats, rats, insects, and the like.[2]

Despite this bit of practical wisdom, however, there is no evidence in Rush's writings that the "passion" of fear is systematically related to his psychiatric observations.

In Griesinger's famous textbook, the second German edition of which appeared in 1861, considerable emphasis was placed programmatically on various psychical causes of mental disease. Griesinger noted especially sudden anger, shock, grief, disappointment, jealousy, and fear, and considers them "the most frequent and the most fertile sources of insanity." Perhaps even more pointed is his footnote: "Guislain found, amongst 100 patients who were admitted in the course of a year, shock or anxiety to be the cause of the insanity in nine instances." [3]

The role of fear in normal life was also underscored by the writings of Darwin and Spencer. The astute clinician and ardent Spencerian theorizer, John Hughlings Jackson, noted in 1867 the organic substratum of fear when, speaking of certain epileptic seizure phenomena, he wrote: "Not a fear of the fit, but fear which comes by itself." He saw fear "in the raw," so to speak, produced directly by certain brain discharges, independent of the patient's situational factors or self reflections.[4]

Interesting in its succinctness is the description which Tuke gave of anxiety in his *Dictionary of Psychological Medicine* (1892) : "Mental distress in expectation of some sorrow or trial. A condition of agitation and depression, with a sensation of tightness and distress in the praecordial region." [5]

It is equally interesting to note that despite its rather modern title, *Lectures on the Diagnosis and Treatment of Functional Nervous Affections* (1868) , by Brown-Sequard, no mention was made of anxiety or any similar affect.[6] Meynert's text of 1885 also omitted any reference to it.[7] And even in the 1957 edition of the *Encyclopaedia Britannica,* anxiety still does not have an independent entry, but is discussed under the headings of hysteria, abnormal psychology, defense mechanisms, psychoanalysis, psychosis, and emotion. Enough to indicate, however, that the nineteenth century was familiar with anxiety and that many psychiatrists and neurologists accorded it a place in the etiology and symptomatology of mental disease although it would be assigned the crucial role in mental disorders only in our own century. Altschule has found a similar importance attached to anxiety by a number of eighteenth century British medical writers.[8]

The major breakthrough, however, which would accord anxiety the most central role in the etiology and symptomatology of mental disorders and which would help establish the idea that our own era is an "Age of Anxiety" came with the study of hysteria. Made a respectable research domain by Charcot, the chaotic phenomena of hysteria began to yield to conceptual understanding, law, and order, at the same rate that the clinical importance of anxiety began to be understood, until it seemed, in Freud's earlier writings, that the primary "model" for anxiety was to be found in hysteria and its allies: traumatic neuroses, anxiety neurosis, and neurasthenia. Where others, including Janet, saw a link between anxiety and hysteria, Freud's perspicacious view saw a near-equation and established at once the dynamic understanding of a syndrome and the dynamics of an emotion.

But what were the phenomena that clinicians dealt with as the essence and primary manifestations of anxiety? For the pre-psychoanalytic psychiatrists they were "states of morbid fear," particularly the phobias and acute panic attacks. Rush's "unreasonable fears" are what we now call phobias, without the embellishment of Greek names. They were also certain phenomena, subjective or objective, of epilepsy, as described by Jackson. For Charcot, Janet, and Freud, they were a wide range of clinical symptoms, such as convulsions involving the most peculiar body contortions, sudden attacks of blindness or tubular vision, insensitivity to pain stimuli on the skin, paralyses of legs or arms, tachycardia, dyspnea, and other gross alterations of vital bodily processes. Or they were "absences" or twilight states which indicated peculiar changes in the level of consciousness. Occasionally they were the bizarre changes in identity and self-awareness associated with multiple personality. And along with all these, there were the seeming simulations of focal brain dysfunctions, such as aphasia, agnosia, apraxia, but without any demonstrable or expected lesions and often with sudden recurrence of normal functioning.

In other words, these phenomena were clinically significant, painful, costly, and disruptive manifestations of an emotion within the sphere of mind-body relations. They were signs and symptoms of profound organismic upheavals which threatened the organization of personalities and which often resulted in permanent or temporary dissolution of any integration thus far achieved.

Moreover the clinician knew that cause and effect relations in such a complicated emotion as anxiety tended to lead to unstoppable chains of reactions, whereby things often went from bad to worse. Even such a non-dynamic thinker as Kraepelin realized that in phobias, for instance, the event which is feared is often precipitated by the very anxiety the patient has for its occurrence, and that subsequent defense reactions can worsen the patient's situation.[9]

In the clinical tradition, moreover, attention is being paid to the continuities between animal nature and human nature. In work on experimental neurosis in animals, the animal is said to experience anxiety, not "just fear." This is in contrast to the attempts by some to reserve the term anxiety for the specifically human experience (man as a symbolic, time-binding being who searches for meaning), and use the word fear for the experiences common to both animals and man.

The correlated processes of the autonomic nervous system are fairly clear: sympathetic discharges which produce accelerated cardiac output, increased blood pressure, rapid breathing, pupil dilation, muscle contractions, and so on, with inhibition of parasympathetic activity. There is also considerable clarity about the immediate psychological correlates or sequelae such as inhibition, restriction of awareness, repression, hypervigilance, disorganization of thought, dissolution of established action patterns, loss of integration. And it is widely recognized that the individual defends himself against the feeling of anxiety by various defense mechanisms, coping devices, homeostatic maneuvers, adaptive processes, or whatever technical term one prefers.

But clinicians are committed to healing and are often distracted from considering carefully the *whole spectrum of intensities* of anxiety. Anxiety becomes clinically relevant precisely when it is a "great anxiety" or extends too long in time and becomes a chronic anxiety or reaches a sudden peak of great intensity as in acute anxiety attacks. It may be that weak and strong intensities of anxiety have very different effects upon the organism, even when both are subjectively experienced as unpleasant. Indeed experimental psychologists and learning theoreticians have pointed out that anxiety (as operationally defined in each experiment) may be conceptualized as a secondary drive and may have a positively motivating effect. On the other hand, learning is more enhanced by anxiety reduction than by anxiety arousal.

Many clinicians, taken off guard, would acknowledge that without some anxiety few persons would prepare themselves for examinations and other important tasks in life. Still on further thought they might argue that an ideally organized person may pass an examination more successfully and deploy his talents better if it were possible for him to prepare himself joyfully, without the least taint of anxious feelings. Such an objection, however, must be checked against experimental findings of studies dealing with the lower end of the spectrum of anxiety intensities. It should not be stated in the form of an unverified opinion, for in that case it may be only an oblique formulation of the speaker's preference for an anxiety-free existence and thus of his value system, which in turn restricts the conceptual realm of the word "anxiety" *for him*. And then one is back in the muddle of semantics, in which different sections of the total spectrum of anxiety intensities receive different verbal labels according to anyone's whims.

Intensity of anxiety is obviously not the whole story. Clinicians have distinguished in another realm (sometimes seen as a special form of anxiety) between guilt *feelings* as psychically real and guilt as morally or objectively real. A somewhat different distinction between the subjective and objective aspects has been made in regard to anxiety, leading to the concept of anxiety as only psychically real, and "realistic fear" (Rush's rational fears) as an appropriate and highly adaptive response to a dangerous object. In this distinction the inside-outside problem plays a part, but also the type and degree of subjective awareness of the experiencer. There are very different theories in regard to the prototypes of anxiety and fear, and one can make attempts to reduce one term to the other by way of genetic analysis. Whether the prototype, however, be fear or anxiety and whether one's emphasis is on intrapsychic conflict or interpersonal conflict, there seems to be basic agreement among most psychiatrists and psychologists that both fear and anxiety, whether rational or irrational, conscious or unconscious, determined from inside or outside are always *unpleasant emotions* which tend to disturb the current equilibrium of the subject.

This very brief survey cannot do justice to the baffling complexities which clinicians and psychologists have perceived in the phenomena of anxiety. There is an immense literature on the subject which concerns itself with such typical chapter headings as: Anxiety and Affect, Anxiety as a Drive State, Anxiety and Learning, Anxiety and Perception, Physiology of Anxiety, and so on, and much in the current literature on ego-psychology is a way of conceptualizing the problems of anxiety. It seems to me, however, that the clinical context has shown preference for defining anxiety as an affect and for appraising its role in personality as disturbing and unpleasant and thus potentially pathogenic.

The Existential-Theological Context

Again in this section our interest lies not in an extensive historical analysis of the term anxiety, but in describing some major contextual meanings of the term anxiety for theologians. It would seem that for this purpose the clock needs to be turned back 120 years to the writings of Kierkegaard. Whether or not he is truly the father of the modern theologians' concern with anxiety is irrelevant here (indeed some people may consider him a brilliant pupil of Augustine) —it is enough that most contemporary theologians who have interested themselves in the problem acknowledge their immense indebtedness to him.

Already from the titles of his books one can see Kierkegaard's preoccupation with the phenomena of anxiety.[10, 11, 12] They cover nearly all the important cognate terms: dread, fear, trembling, despair, sickness. But on opening his works one can easily see that he writes as a philosopher and a theologian, not as a clinician, despite his astute observations and psychological mindedness. He certainly rejected the language of science, preferring to formulate his thoughts in paradoxes, parables, learned discourses, and extremely condensed dialectic propositions. "Dread is a sympathetic antipathy and an antipathetic sympathy." "What effect does nothing produce? It begets dread." "Dread is the reality of freedom as possibility anterior to possibility." Indeed how different from Freud's, "Missing someone who is loved and longed for is the key to an understanding of anxiety." [13]

Is Kierkegaard in the quoted phrases talking about the same thing that the psychiatrists of his day and later saw in the mental hospitals? Did he, while writing about dread, see people in panic, in the throes of convulsions, in dereistic states, in severe hypochondriasis, in *pavor nocturnus,* in phobias, or in severe depression, threatening suicide? Perhaps he did see a connection at some profound level of understanding (after all, he himself and some of his relatives offered some noteworthy examples of temporary mental derangement [14]) but I am afraid his real models lay elsewhere and were quite different. I think he thought and wrote, at least in part, as a shrewdly observing pastor (despite his rejection of the office) and with much pastoral "feel" for a tragic human situation; and also as a driven, demanding, hard-hitting prophet who could be the strictest taskmaster when facing the inertia of a nominally Christian crowd. He thought as a sort of intellectual evangelist, calling people to become Christians. His most technical manuscript, the "Concluding Unscientific Postscript" ended precisely with this: "What it is to become a Christian"—directed at the registered church members of his day.[15]

If a kind of evangelism, in the best and cleverest sense of the word, was indeed Kierkegaard's overruling perspective on all things, it is to be expected that he would discuss anxiety and its cognates in the context of the major theological questions about man: his creatureliness, his Fall, the rebellious arrogance of sin, and his freedom and destiny. This was precisely what he did. Do not be mistaken by the word "sickness" in *The Sickness unto Death*—it has very little to do with illness but very much to do with sin. And so with *Fear and Trembling,* which is really a book about ethics: "In the story of Abraham we find such a paradox. His relation to Isaac, ethically expressed, is this: that the father should love the son. This ethical relation is reduced to a relative position in contrast with the absolute relation to God." It is a book about temptation (Luther's *Anfechtung*) and obedience. As a matter of fact, a careful reading of these two works is not likely to make one anxious or depressed, for despite the tremendously rich meanings of the words "fear" and "despair" which flow from Kierkegaard's sharp pen, they carry very little true affect. They may make us pensive, brooding, ill at ease with ourselves; they may spur us on to self-examination; they may put us into a mood (how Kierkegaard hated that word!) of reverence; but they do not bring us into a state of empathy with heroes or

sinners suffering from pangs of guilt or anxiety. On the contrary—
the texts give rich intellectual satisfactions. They are very different from Jonathan Edwards' famous sermon on "Sinners in the
Hand of an Angry God," which apparently had the power to
throw the listeners into convulsions.

Kierkegaard entertained a *religious* or, more accurately, a Christian view of anxiety in which the doctrine of original sin must
first be affirmed. He saw anxiety as a correlate of human freedom,
that is, the freedom to act consciously and voluntarily upon one's
acquired knowledge of good and evil. Anxiety or the "dizziness
of freedom" is a necessary part, if not the essence, of the religious
crisis situation through which a man grows (or leaps) out of his
innocence into the full realization that he is a sinner before God
and has always wanted to be just that.

And here is the point at which the clinician may become
baffled over this formulation: Though Kierkegaard admitted that
anxiety is painful and that most people will *naturally* do anything to prevent their experiencing it (which is precisely what
keeps man in a state of nature, that is, innocence), he also entertained the notion: "the more freedom, the more anxiety" and
vice versa. In clinical experience, however, anxiety is always
found to *limit* freedom, because it is a disturbing affect. Only
when anxiety is reduced and worked through can freedom increase.

I think one has to be aware of the fact that Kierkegaard dealt
with a special anxiety, a special freedom, and a special form of
psychic equilibrium or integration. Because of his prior endorse-
ment of the doctrine of original sin he must proclaim that most,
if not all, human integration, health, peace of mind, and so on are
at heart only a false tranquillity and a sham existence. In his eyes,
almost everyone was too inert, too bourgeois, too sedate and satisfied and therefore must be *made anxious,* so as to move from
vegetating into true being. Kierkegaard is one of James's twice-
born men and what he did was to challenge all others to be born
again. He urged them to undergo a new "birth trauma" by pass-
ing through the *"angustia"* of coming to recognize one's creature-

liness before God. Now whereas in Rank's birth trauma theory, espoused as one model of primary anxiety by Freud, the primary anxiety was causal and lies in the past, in Kierkegaard's "birth trauma" theory the primary anxiety seemed to be teleological and opened vistas into a life yet to come.

But can an affect be teleological? And will anyone being asked to become anxious obediently follow suit? Surely one can be *made* anxious or be *forced* into anxiety, but that always happens by a present fact or thought of threat and danger. Affects belong to the archaic inheritance of man and belong to his instinctual equipment. Their power consists precisely in their long past, racially and individually, and their usefulness in their application to present realities. My contention is that teleological forces in man are not affects, but values, principles, ideals, and goals. And it seems to me that Kierkegaard dealt indeed with anxiety and freedom as values. It is even rather difficult to sort out from his writings which of the two he valued more highly: anxiety or freedom.

At this point it is interesting to look a hundred years ahead and consider what Heidegger did with anxiety.[16] He literally implored and exhorted people to have anxiety, not in order that they *gain* freedom (so that anxiety might simply be the dear price of the precious good of freedom), but just to *have* anxiety heroically, irrespective of any gain other than the intellectual honesty of having stared nothingness in the face. This is an honesty we owe to ourselves. *Anxiety here becomes a cognitive state, an intellectual state of great lucidity. It is revealing, uncovering;* it gives access to a certain depth level of reality.

I do not think Kierkegaard went that far, but he did see anxiety, among other things, as *a form of knowing.* He could and must put it that way because his religious epistemology stated that knowledge of man co-varies with the knowledge of God: Man can know himself only to the extent that he knows God. This God, however, is known not as a cold concept, but in awe, dread, fear, and trembling. And man does not owe it to himself to know his situation—he owes it to God, who as his Maker demands it from him. Anxiety then is bound up with the duty of every man to *assess* himself, to take stock of his situation, and to *become aware* of his ultimate dependency upon his Maker. It *reveals* the contingency of human existence. But once this is seen, anxiety becomes also something one has to put up with as the "wages of sin." Thus evaluated it turns into guilt, not guilt feelings, but real guiltiness. It has become a moral form of knowing, a kind of self-evaluation. In this new perspective "anxiety-guilt" becomes appropriated as a necessary and inalienable condition of the fallen creature. And to the extent that such appropriation takes place, anxiety is met by the counterforces of grace which give courage and comfort and thereby "take the sting out of it."

In dialectic writings, however, the logical and time relations of the *prius* to the *secundus* are obscured. When Kierkegaard and Heidegger stressed the revelatory nature of anxiety, one cannot be sure whether anxiety is meant to lead to knowledge or knowledge of a certain sort to anxiety. Despite some of his dark utterances, Kierkegaard's religious premises convince me that knowledge of one's contingency, however achieved, is more likely to be cause than effect of the "anxiety-guilt" he described.

Largely following in Kierkegaard's footsteps, Reinhold Niebuhr also put anxiety in the context of original sin and its consequences.[17] Anxiety is the inevitable concomitant of freedom and finiteness. It has its positive and negative aspects. On the one hand it may lead to the creative act of clearly recognizing the deeper and truer situation of man as a rebellious and proud creature; on the other hand it is, given the situation of original *sin,* the great temptress which seduces man to more *sins.*

In Niebuhr's use, the word "anxiety" has often the connotation of "anxiousness *about.*" Particularly in his concrete examples of anxiety the meaning of his word anxiety comes close to that of Heidegger's *Sorge (cura)* , in the sense of an *apprehensive concern* or *preoccupation with.*[18] Although this does not rule out an affective tone, it places considerable emphasis on cognitive aspects, particularly when its possible positive consequences (creativity) are taken into account.

Niebuhr finds it difficult to make a neat separation between constructive and destructive aspects of anxiety. He clearly sees that both are present and that it would be arbitrary to set up a strict demarcation between the two. It would seem, however, that he tends to give the stronger weight to the negative aspects when he states: "Without freedom from anxiety man is so enmeshed in the vicious circle of egocentricity, so concerned about himself, that he cannot release himself for the adventure of love." [19] I think that in this statement anxiety is taken in the meaning of an inhibiting force which fails to give proper scope to perception and knowledge—precisely what psychologists would ascribe to affect. It has a blinding effect, it produces a "cloud of unknowing." Here seems to be one lead, then, *that there may be a correlation between a positive evaluation of anxiety and seeing it as a cognition and a negative evaluation of anxiety and seeing it as an affect.* Now under what circumstances can anxiety be knowledge-producing? And what sort of knowledge, if any, can anxiety evolve? Since most philosophers and theologians who have concerned themselves with anxiety have been existentialists (perhaps they have been called existentialists precisely because of that concern!) their answer has been in the main that anxiety can produce knowledge about man's ontological status. It is admittedly not helpful in solving mathematical puzzles; it isn't of use in winning a chess game; it does not foster a mechanic's accuracy and adroitness in handling his tools. The knowledge it may give is of a special class: man's ontic relations to freedom, dependency, the Ground of Being, his choice of absolutes, and his options for spiritual growth or stagnation. And if anxiety can produce such knowledge (which is still by no means demonstrated) it is very likely to do so via the ontological negative (but sometimes metaphysical positive) of "nonbeing." Prior to any decision which may affirm "being" there has to be the stark vision of death and its various symbolic representations. Cognitive clarity about the inescapability of death in all its forms (and about one's alignment hitherto with the "Prince of Death"—evil, sin, sloth, stagnation, rebellious denial of God, proud aspirations, and so on) is the first condition that may eventually lead to the "leap of faith" in which one "chooses" the better option of a modest, limited existence which is warmed by a realization of one's love-borne and divinely given creatureliness or to the bitter choice of just heroically accepting one's fate *sans rancune*. It is to be noted that the knowledge thus engendered is not a knowledge of cold hard facts or interesting intellectual tidbits but a knowledge of values as the guiding principles of one's own life.

But the more pointed question is now whether anxiety can indeed produce even this first cognitive result of a lucid awareness of one's own finiteness. At this junction the thought of Tillich becomes relevant to my thesis. Basic to Tillich's ontology of anxiety is the position that the terms "being" and "nonbeing" be taken dynamically, after the Heraclitean model of change and the biological model of life.[20] Being thus includes becoming, and nonbeing refers to nonbecoming with the result that nonbeing has ontological status and relevance.

Within this framework, anxiety is defined as "the state in which a being is aware of its possible nonbeing." This implies a particularized, ego-involved knowing of one's own finitude; an awareness of "not being able to preserve one's own being." It is a condition that cannot be countered by anything. It is a basic given of human existence, and therefore existential anxiety. Since it cannot be eliminated or mitigated by something else it tends to abolish itself, so to speak, by generating specific fears which can then be met by courage.

What, in experiential terms, is this so-called existential anxiety? Does it have psychological content? Tillich refers to introspective reports by a few heroes of the spirit who have described it as an "unimaginable horror," a "night of the soul," or a "great disgust." While these terms seem rather emotional at first glance, we should not be fooled by them into believing that, therefore, the state to which they refer is in itself an emotion. It seems to me that precisely its definition as "ontic" or "existential" takes this kind of anxiety out of the academic categories of psychology. Ontic states cannot be defined as part processes of psychological functioning; they are *prior* to any psychological (or sociological, biochemical, or other scientific) specificity. Existential anxiety is neither emotion, intellection, action, memory, willing, ideation nor any other item in the psychological index.

Tillich sees the metamorphosis of anxiety into fear as a spontaneous process, aided by cultural conditions. The two remain related: "The sting of fear is anxiety, and anxiety strives toward fear." Is existential anxiety thus "pure sting"? Apparently not, for its usual correlates such as pain, loss, feeling of rejection, dying, and so on are attributed by Tillich to fear. Perhaps we may say that existential anxiety is *anticipation of a terminus,* yet without clarity about its form, nature, or quality. The only concept which psychologists may think of in this connection is the objectless but ego-involved state described by the Wuerzburg School as *Bewusstseinslage* or "determining tendency" and perhaps Titchener's "imageless thought." It is important to realize that those concepts were generated from research in problem solving, willing and patterning of associations in the stream of thought. I am tempted to translate Tillich's proposition about existential anxiety now as: "An imageless anticipation or *Bewusstseinslage* of nothing, with the feeling that one is delivered to it [nothing] without help." Note that the first clause describes a bare minimum of cognitive content. This may refer to an ontic awareness, but it is not yet existential *anxiety.* Anxiety comes in the second clause, when a feeling of "being delivered unto" is described. The question is whether the second clause may be reduced to the first as effect and cause and whether the ontic awareness of nothing is always responded to, or followed by, the feeling of being delivered unto it in the sense of the affect of anxiety. A similar critical question has been raised by Kaufmann about Heidegger's assertion that anxiety is the primary reaction to Being-in-the-world.[21] One is again faced with the inherent obscurity of dialectic reasoning to which I alluded above.

Fairly late in his career as an investigator, Freud said: "The question of the stuff out of which anxiety is made loses interest for us." [22] But ontologists tend to be bolder than scientists and some of them have tried to specify the "stuff" of anxiety. In doing so, however, they may have offered only a flimsy abstract construct. Particularly when ontology is practised with the help of the phenomenological method, such a result is to be expected. An "eidetic reduction" is perhaps possible when one is seated comfortably behind one's desk, detached from the worries and distractions of everyday life, and when one has chosen the mathematical idea of number, the phenomena of color vision, or the forms of sculpture for one's subject matter. But for a study of the subjective side of anxiety one needs the live experience of anxiety and this involves the paradoxical problem that the anxious person or any person in a state of anxiety is the least apt or able to make a phenomenological study of anxiety. At the risk of being accused of psychologism, I would suggest that the shortcoming of many philosophers and theologians of anxiety lies precisely in their not having seen this simple (I am tempted to say basic if the term were not preempted by ontology) psychological fact.

I introduced this section by asking whether anxiety (as defined by some theologians) can indeed produce the cognitive result of a lucid awareness of one's own finiteness. It has now become obvious that in all probability anxiety leads to no such result. Tillich indeed seems to propose that the relations be reversed: The awareness of nothingness generates existential anxiety and this existential anxiety—to the degree that it is *felt*—dissolves itself into specific fears which may be dealt with by various manipulations which imply the counter-attitude of courage. Existential anxiety is thus always self-eliminating, and in arguing backwards from felt or observed fears to a presupposed existential anxiety the latter turns out to be not an affect at all but at best an extremely vague, almost contentless, diffuse state of awareness, no more than a *Bewusstseinslage*. Tillich is quite aware of the rarity of existential anxiety. It may occur in "extreme situations," "rare occasions," or in some people, not at all.[23]

Tentative Conclusions

And now one may return to one of Tillich's *causes célèbres:* Luther. I do not think that Luther had an "unimaginable horror" over nothingness, nor that he threw his inkwell at nonbeing. His "void of nothingness," like the "dark night of the soul" of many mystics, was filled with visions of psychically real, almost substantial, actually threatening *beings* such as the devil and his cohorts. The existential choice situation for Kierkegaard was not between something or nothing, but between God and Devil, God and flesh, good and evil portrayed, between becoming one type of man or another type of man. If there is a passionate experience of passion there is always an object of passion. Not that one is always conscious of this object. We must maintain, however, the hypothesis that the object is there, somewhere in one's memory.

Contrary to Kierkegaard's verbal formulations, dread is not produced by nothing. It is produced by a threatening substance or the image thereof. The heart of the matter has often been obscured by poorly chosen words plus the reifications of abstractions, suggesting that there is "something there." For example, while nothingness and death may have much in common, there is an important difference between nothingness and dying, just as there is between death and dying. It is easy to contemplate death and the very thought of it has given rise to beautiful literary and philosophical works, which the reader can absorb without negative feelings. They can even be read with gusto by the aesthete. But what really *gives us the shivers* is to confront the process of dying or to anticipate it imaginatively in ourselves. Its horror is the horror of pain and what it feels like to fall apart.

There is a beautiful French proverb: *"Partir, c'est mourir un peu,"* which one may translate literally as: "Taking leave is dying a little." It relates the experience of departure, loss, detachment, and thus also of the "longing for the lost object" to the anticipated horrors of dying, the latter being the model for the former. Dying is not an abstract definition nor simply a "state." It is the painful, gruesome decomposition of the psychosomatic unit which we are. It is a process, among others, of the body in its concreteness with its *sensations* of anxiety in the gut, the heart, the throat, the joints, the muscles. Freud was undoubtedly correct when he treated anxiety as an affect and saw its prototype in the trauma of birth.

I think it is matched by a "telotype" which I would describe as the trauma of dying—not the contemplation of death or nothing or "ashes" or "dust," but dying.

My conclusions are only tentative. To aim at anything more would be presumptuous, for anxiety is enigmatic enough and will continue to baffle the keenest minds. But I hope it will be noted that my proposition is not an ontological speculation but a psychological inference with concrete referents in the lifetime of the individual. Dying is still an act of living and thus within the scope of psychology. Ontologies of anxiety can never do justice to the concrete bodily reality of *felt* anxiety as an unpleasant and disturbing affect, because in ontology the "stuff" of life is evaporated. Perhaps here lies also a hint about the relations between ontology and psychology. While in the hierarchy of systematic thinking ontology should precede psychology, as ontology supposedly precedes everything, this relation may have to be reversed when ontology takes the special course, as it has done since Heidegger, of defining Being via the experiences of "being human."

Existential anxiety, so-called, is not really an affect. It is only a misused term which has come up when philosophers and theologians have tried to fit human realities into the highest possible philosophical abstractions, with the n-th degree of conceptual reductionism. This always tends to end up in a hopeless syncretism where everything is equated with everything, without specificity in anything, but with the false glamour of an ultimate truth captured.

Anxiety can be called existential only in the sense that it is felt centrally, demonstrated psychosomatically, experienced unpleasantly, and reacted to holistically. But this is true of all anxiety and of all negative affects. Thus experienced, there is no categorical difference between existential anxiety and any other anxiety. Existential anxiety cannot form the basis of a complaint, nor can it be the object of healing. The moment any anxiety is described as a concrete experience it is an affect.

We have seen that the term anxiety and its cognates can be used in very different contexts and that their meanings are heavily determined by the philosophical and scientific presuppositions of their users. Though my own views are not wholly unbiased, I have made an effort to enter into the meanings of anxiety for various authors via their contextual referents. Two different classes of interpretations were found: a predominantly affective and a predominantly cognitive group of definitions. There is also a strong suggestion that those who espouse a cognitive interpretation tend to evaluate anxiety positively, whereas those who favor an affective definition tend to evaluate anxiety negatively. It would only be trite to suggest that the truth might lie in the middle.

References

1. Thomas Stephen Szasz, *Pain and Pleasure; A Study of Bodily Feelings* (New York: Basic Books Inc., Publishers, 1957).
2. B. Rush, *Medical Inquiries and Observations upon the Diseases of the Mind* (3rd ed.; Philadelphia: Johnson & Warner et al., 1927).
3. W. Griesinger, *Mental Pathology and Therapeutics*, trans. C. Lockhart Robertson and James Rutherford (2nd ed.; London: The New Sydenham Society, 1867), p. 165.
4. John Hughlings Jackson, "Remarks on Evolution and Dissolution of the Nervous System," *Journal of Mental Science*, April 1867; also in *Jackson, Selected Writings*, eds. James Taylor et al (2 vols.; New York, Basic Books, Inc., Publishers, 1958).
5. Daniel Hack Tuke, *A Dictionary of Psychological Medicine* (Philadelphia: P. Blakiston, Son & Company, 1892).
6. C. E. Brown-Sequard, *Lectures on the Diagnosis and Treatment of Functional Nervous Affections* (Philadelphia, J. B. Lippincott & Co., 1868).
7. Th. Meynert, *Psychiatry; A Clinical Treatise on Diseases of the Forebrain*, trans. B. Sachs (New York-London: G. P. Putnam's Sons, 1885).
8. Mark Davis and Evelyn Russ Altschule, *Roots of Modern Psychiatry; Essays in the History of Modern Psychiatry* (New York: Grune & Stratton, Inc., 1957).
9. Emil Kraepelin, *Psychiatrie*, (Leipzig: Barth, 1915) Vol. IV.
10. Sören Kierkegaard, *Fear and Trembling*, trans. Walter Lowrie (New York: Doubleday & Company, Inc., 1954).
11. Kierkegaard, *The Concept of Dread*, trans. Walter Lowrie (Princeton: Princeton University Press, 1944). Used by permission.
12. Kierkegaard, *The Sickness unto Death*, trans. Walter Lowrie (New York: Doubleday & Company, Inc., 1954).
13. Sigmund Freud, "Inhibitions, Symptoms and Anxiety," *Standard Edition of the Complete Psychological Works of Sigmund Freud*, general ed. and trans. James Strachey (24 vols.; New York: The Macmillan Co., 1961). Used by permission of The Hogarth Press and Basic Books, Inc. XX, 87-174.

14. E. Weigert, "Sören Kierkegaard's Mood Swings," *International Journal of Psycho-Analysis*, 1960, XXI, 521-25.
15. Kierkegaard, "Concluding Unscientific Postscript," *A Kierkegaard Anthology*, ed. Robert Bretall (Princeton: Princeton University Press, 1947).
16. Martin Heidegger, *Sein und Zeit* (Halle a.d.s.: Max Niemeyer Verlag, 1935).
17. Reinhold Niebuhr, *The Nature and Destiny of Man; A Christian Interpretation* (2 vols.; New York: Charles Scribner's Sons, 1941). Vol. I.
18. *Ibid.*, pp. 184-85.
19. *Ibid.*, p. 272.
20. Paul Tillich, *The Courage To Be* (New Haven: Yale University Press, 1952). Used by permission.
21. W. Kaufmann, "Existentialism and Death," in *The Meaning of Death*, ed. Herman Feifel (New York: McGraw-Hill Book Co., Inc., 1959).
22. Freud, *New Introductory Lectures on Psycho-Analysis*, trans, W. J. H. Sprott (New York: W. W. Norton and Company, Inc., 1933.) Used by permission. Ch. iv.
23. Tillich, *op. cit.*, pp. 56-57.

Epilogue

Seward Hiltner

It was just a generation ago that Freud declared the understanding of anxiety to be in a state of flux and change. Is this still the situation? Is the meaning of anxiety unclear within psychiatry and within theology (and within other interested fields), as well as among the several interested disciplines? The answer seems to be yes to all these questions, despite much good work and thought that has taken place including, I believe, the provocative discussions in the present volume.

As I worked with my co-editor, Karl Menninger, with all the contributors and especially with Paul W. Pruyser, with members of the Publications Department of The Menninger Foundation, and with a helpful Abingdon Press editor, I found myself ever more appreciative of the work of our contributors and what their chapters accomplish in the direction of clarifying the meaning and processes of anxiety. Yet at the same time I found them so stimulating my own constructive thought on the subject that I became reluctant to leave the last word with them.

As my fantasies collected, leading finally to this epilogue, I alternated between thinking that what I had to add was trite and that it was integrative in a revolutionary way. What finally made me decide to write it was that even my most expansive oral presentations of the ideas were welcomed, not as "the" integrating answer to the problem but as possibly moving us a step closer toward such an answer. This discussion appears as an epilogue because it did not, as do all the chapters, emerge directly from the Gallahue Conference. The epilogue form, in addition, has left me unconstrained to confine my discussion to points mentioned previously in the volume, and thus has permitted my imagination to rove all over the arena of anxiety.

The reader should take this epilogue as an honest but preliminary and ruminative attempt to make one additional move toward constructing a unified theory of anxiety. He will, I trust, recognize that the effort is serious. Yet I hope he will recognize also that I have set limits upon the degree of seriousness with which my discussion should be interpreted, and will see the occasional bits of lightness or playfulness not as flippancies but as reminders to myself to be serious but not ponderous or pretentious.

Especially as I have reread the chapters of this volume and some other basic materials like Freud's and Kierkegaard's, I find this question coming to the fore: In what *context* does anxiety appear? Another way to put the same question is: Within what concrete life process does anxiety appear as a part or aspect?

So put, this is a "dumb question." Any right-minded Freudian or existentialist or Christian or social scientist knows—but does he? Is it possible that some at least of the problems of theorizing integratedly about anxiety are less a matter of accuracy of observation than of the setting in which the observations are viewed? Could there be a *common* setting or context perhaps in spite of the varying concerns of such investigators as psychiatrists and theologians? Could it be that the integrative problem is not with the "facts"—at least for anyone sufficiently concerned to get the facts from the several disciplines—but with the context in which those facts are viewed? Could each discipline be so slanting its conception of context that it obscures the common dimensions of context? I have come to believe so and, without staking my future on the resulting reflections, I want to try to illuminate this contextual problem.

Regardless of their fields of specialization, all the authorities that have been cited in this book and our authors are agreed on one point which is, however, not explicitly mentioned, no doubt because it seems so obvious and obtrusive. This point is that anxiety—whether conceived as signal, as affect, as alertness, or as confrontation—is involved in a total process that involves danger or challenge, or the response to danger or challenge. May it be clarifying if, temporarily, we set aside the question of precisely what anxiety is, and instead, review the general facts about the human response to danger or challenge?

This leads us first to the nature of emotion as physiologists elucidated it earlier in this century. Emotion, they said, is an automatic process within the organism whereby it mobilizes itself to try to meet danger or challenge. At the level of gross physiological change (like increased heart beat or endocrinological activity), there is not much difference whether one is being mobilized to attack or to flee the source of danger, although of course there is a radical difference in the psychology of these two responses. Even milder excitation, like a momentary startle or like tender feelings for another person, shows measurable changes to the physiologist. Thus mild emotion and stark emotion exist on a continuum of a sort from the physiologist's point of view; from the point of view of what they do to the organism regarded psychologically, however, there is a radical difference. Mild emotion seems like the seasoning of psychic life. If a person never experienced it, life as relatedness to other persons and things would lose its savor. And it can appear, one may say, because the normal tone is resumed easily after each excitation.

With stark or gross emotion, the situation is different. This mobilizing apparatus came into being in man's evolution when the gross dangers and challenges were of a kind that could be met by fight or flight, such as stalking the animal to kill it for meat or dashing up a tree or into a cave to evade its jaws. When an early man became grossly emotional and fought or fled from his animal, and was successful either way, he thereby discharged the energy that the mobilization process had added to his routine supply; and after a bit of time for his breath and blood pressure to come back to normal, he was the same as before excitation began. Thus the emotional apparatus for dealing with gross danger or challenge was for earlier man (so long as he did not get killed in his fight or flight) effective.

Manifestly the kinds of dangers and challenges confronted by man in culture and civilization are seldom of the gross type. Very few of them require or even permit the discharge of the added physiological energy made available automatically, whether one wants it or not, upon the perception of a serious danger or challenge. The car driver suddenly confronted with the very narrow bridge, discussed in the second chapter, is an illustration of this difference. When he perceives the narrow bridge, his body mobilizes as if he were to hack it down or run away from it; yet what he must do to meet this danger is neither of those things, but is much more careful steering of his car. He is mobilized for one kind of danger while he actually encounters another kind. It may even be (at least in some instances) that the kind of mobilization that takes place is maladaptive to the kind of danger he confronts, as when a person "freezes" to the controls. Whether or not that is so in particular instances, it is certain that not every element in the emotional mobilization process is automatically helpful in meeting the danger or challenge; and that, therefore, the person goes through a lifetime of literal emotional "self-education" in which he selects from the total mobilization process those aspects that assist adaptation (to his kind of danger) and tries to neutralize the effect of others. In human life the resulting patterns become very complex indeed.

Let us suppose that our car driver approaching the bridge has been a master at emotional self-education, and that he uses the alerting aspects of his emotional mobilization to perceive the dimensions of the bridge more accurately but suppresses other aspects of the mobilization that might make him throw up his hands or jam on the accelerator or the brake—and that, thereby, he negotiates the bridge successfully. If so, he has really met successfully *two* dangers; the bridge on the one hand, and the maladaptive (to this danger) aspects of his emotional mobilization on the other hand.

But what happens after that? If he is wise, we noted, he will roll to a stop in a half mile or so, relax for a bit or, perhaps better, get out and walk around. Even though he neutralized, so far as the bridge danger was concerned, those aspects of his mobilization not helpful in meeting bridges, his adaptive action did not "use up" the extra energy mobilized automatically by his emotion. Unless he gets his emotional level back to near normal, there will be extra wear and tear on his organism. And when the emotional level remains considerably above normal over a period of time, with much excitation undischarged, then the perceptual field, psychologically considered, is considerably altered. It may be that one comes consciously to feel "excited"; but as the excitation and the feeling persist, one regards this feeling as normal, when it is not—as if the standing car with the racing motor were normal for cars at rest. More often, the awareness of the excitation (when there is no longer a danger to fight, or so it seems) is itself unpleasant, or would be if one felt or registered it; so that, by analogy with the standing car of which the motor is racing, he no longer hears the motor. If we ask the first man whether he feels excited, he says yes; if the second man, he says no. Both men have problems, but the first is closer to reality than the second, and both men's problems stem from the same basic process.

In order to make clear the fundamental psychological process that goes on in the human organism when confronting serious danger or challenge, I have run some risk of slanting our concern away from the crucial issues about anxiety. The two men just mentioned, for example, may have nearly the same thing going on in them physiologically, but subjectively and psychically very different processes have begun to take place within them. Or even though fear and rage have quite similar physiological actions, their subjective feeling is radically different. From the uniquely human point of view, these differences are enormously significant. Our stress on the physiology of excitation ought not, therefore, to be seen as a homogenizing of subjective psychic experience.

We may now turn to a quick summary of what has emerged from the psychological and psychiatric points of view concerning the total human process of confronting danger or challenge. The previous discussion has already shown not only that there are degrees of using the emotional mobilization apparatus for adaptive (or nonadaptive) purposes, but also that such ways may or may not be learned in the course of life experience. Second, it has shown not only that there may be degrees of congruence between what one feels subjectively and what is actually going on inside, but also that the subjective quality of the feeling may alter radically (through repression and the like). One may be excited and yet unaware of it.

A third important point, from a psychological point of view, concerns perception of dangers or challenges *as* dangers or challenges, including the interpretation of nondangerous things as dangerous, the interpretation of dangerous things as nondangerous, the evaluation of mildly dangerous things as severe threats, and the appraisal of severe dangers as only mild obstacles.

Very complex factors influence the person's perception of danger or challenge: his original temperament, his culture and his status within it, his immediate interpersonal environment, his intelligence and its specific nature, his sex as male or female, his education formal and informal, and the specific historical events, traumas, and decisions of his actual life experience. Indeed a very great deal of psychology and psychiatry are designed to try to sort out the relative importance of all these and other factors as they come to influence what and how the person perceives persons, including himself, and other people, events, and things. What he does or does not come to interpret as danger or challenge is, thus, not a mere matter of objectively severe threat or lure but is also a reflection of his individuality and his individual experience. *When* the process of emotional mobilization does or does not go into action is as important to understanding the entire process of response to danger or challenge as is the question of how it operates once it goes to work. If it may be irrelevant in both directions, that fact is as important an aspect of the pathology of response to threat or lure as is running when one should fight or fighting when he should run.

We shall mention only one more point from the psychological point of view. This is that there come to be characteristic overall ways by which human beings approach danger or challenge, and that some of these ways contain more flexibility, freedom, adaptive relevance, and effectiveness than do others. When the characteristic pattern, as in a severely disorganized person, reaches a high degree of rigidity, we tend to think of it as "defense," forgetting that it is also a blind attempt to adapt under severe pressure and with limited resources. When the characteristic pattern, on the other hand, is in a creative and socially contributive person, we tend to think of his pattern as "constructive adaptation," forgetting that it is also built up of a happy variety of flexible and relevant defenses.

From such criteria as mental health, social usefulness, personal happiness, or perceptual integrity, the second person is indeed different from the first. But this difference should not obscure our recognition that both men are responding to danger or challenge according to characteristic patterns which (in all kinds of ways) have been learned, and that something deep in both men is trying to use the resources it has for adaptive purposes, perhaps striving all the more strenuously in the man who is temporarily unsuccessful than in the other. Thus description of the characteristic pattern is important; but it remains incomplete without concomitant description of what Jung would call its "shadow" side—in the ill person, the strength of the underlying will to health, and in the creative person, the relative strength of his fixations and regressions.

In very brief summary, we have now examined the process by which the human being confronts or responds to danger or challenge from the overall perspectives of physiology and of psychology. What about theology? Does it have a perspective upon this process, or is it recreant to the theological concern to put the question in this way?

On the face of it, theology has seemed to be concerned with the process by which *some kinds* of danger and challenge may be met, rather than with the process relating to danger and challenge in general. Bereavement, death, finitude, sin, guilt, alienation, social bondage, injustice—these have been the dangers and challenges *par excellence* with which theology has been concerned. Paul Tillich has rendered the meaning of all these things collectively as "ultimate concern." In a sense that the English language finds difficult to describe, they *are* "ultimate." Perhaps one can hazard that their ultimacy means their decisiveness, their one-way-or-the-otherness, about human fate and destiny. What one does and feels and thinks about them affects *decisively* everything else, large and small, in all the remainder of his life. "Decisive" comes from the Latin word that means "cut off"; hence that which has a "decisive" effect is that which "cuts off" what would otherwise be possible or influential. How a man looks at his approaching mortality, said Tillich as noted in chap. III, affects his entire life. What it "cuts off" is any notion that he can solve this problem by having no imagination about his mortality.

Jewish and Christian theologians, Stoics, and atheistic existentialists all agree that men should confront the ultimate or decisive dangers or challenges, and not act as if these would take care of themselves in the sweet bye and bye. Of course they differ from one another on what is to be found when the hard look is taken. But all are equally against the Philistines, who would ask only the questions they can answer surely, comfortably, or with the help of a scientific or eschatological "some day."

Strangely enough, on the process of confronting ultimate danger and challenge, theologians, Stoics, and existentialists (even Sartre) are agreed except for the final stages. All begin by denying the greater importance of the obtrusively proximate. "Tell me the nature of the god a man believes in or denies, and I will tell you how he rears his children, deals with his neighbor, expresses his sexual impulses, and contributes to peace or to war." This anonymous quotation is a challenge to some genius of a test constructor, but its point is inherent in theology and in such corollary points of view as existentialism and Stoicism. Obtrusive proximity (such as whether you beat your wife, what you do with the residues of the Oedipus complex, or how you ask the boss for a raise) may be, say all these points of view, much more affected by apparently (but not actually) more remote concerns (such as awareness of sinfulness or of mortality or gratitude for God's grace) than any superficial examination could show. Do not, therefore, they continue, so narrow your perspective that you recognize no danger or challenge beyond the next twenty minutes or beyond the family of origin or the country of devotion or the profession of commitment. The apparently remote may be the decisively proximate—from a valuational point of view.

Having established that the human being must confront directly his finitude, mortality, and guilt (and not just hunger, lions and tigers, Oedipus complex, the boss, or sibling rivalry), where does theology (and Stoicism in its modern and ancient forms) go from there? If these are the real dangers and challenges, does it say anything about the process of meeting and dealing with them (in its CAPITAL LETTER FORM) that makes contact with or supplements what we have already learned (in lowercase letters) from physiology, psychology, and psychiatry? I believe it does.

Beyond establishing the proximity of the apparently remote and advising honesty rather than evasion in dealing with it, theology notes the extreme difficulty of these first steps. What makes it possible to take them, it continues, is something outside the ordinary—whether this be conceived by Christian theology as grace or by Stoicism and existentialism as the imaginative acknowledgment of necessity. Sartre's injunction is, finally, to a defiant and courageous kind of nobility: Are you man or mouse? Ancient Stoicism was similarly noble in intent and actually more noble in its language. Christian theology is rather less grim-lipped about what is going on. Its mood is gratitude rather than defiance. While courage is a common denominator, there is an immense attitudinal difference between confronting danger because you'd look silly if you didn't and confronting it because you acknowledge that you have, all unmeritedly, been given the strength to do so by your very Creator.

It should not escape our notice that there are equal temptations

151

to distortion in conscious attitudes of gratitude and of defiance. Defiance asserts integrity *in spite of,* and its temptation is like that of the self-made man who barely acknowledges that he had a mother, was once a fetus, or is dependent on anyone or anything. Gratitude may slip, by imperceptible stages, not only into the anticipation of future favors (as the proverb has it) but also into a passive dependency that takes alertness and awareness out of the stream of actual life, and that substitutes for them a kind of piously numbed acquiescence. Nevertheless in genuine gratitude there is a penetrating apprehension about the true nature of the process of meeting danger and challenge. To quote a wag's phrases, this is not a predilection for pie in the sky (wish-fulfillment) but a readiness to discern the sky in the pie (objectively, the acknowledgment of divine providence; subjectively, gratitude). If God were not already at work—work about redemption, reconciliation, salvation, and fulfillment—there would be: (1) no capacity to acknowledge the *real* dangers, which otherwise seem remote; (2) no source of special strength with which to confront them, and they have special power since they are "ultimate"; (3) no gratitude for being pulled from the abyss but instead a defiant preoccupation with the non-level character of existence; (4) no courage-empowered imagination that can plan and envision even when its present circumstances limit its action to standing.

In terms of relevance and of attitude, then, the theological disciplines do say something about the human process of confronting and dealing with danger and challenge that makes connection with and supplements what we have observed from physiology, psychology, and psychiatry. Yet it must also be acknowledged that theology has generally not attempted to be analytical (especially clinically) in the same sense as these other studies. Hence the identification of relatedness and difference is a difficult task. The capital letters of theology, which are rather like headlines, are suspect of being written by almost anyone but the reporter who actually covered and wrote up the concrete story! Being also a very human enterprise, theology is peculiarly tempted to enter what *The New Yorker* magazine sometimes calls "Infatuated with Sound of Own Words" department, forgetting that revelation gives it no edge on *truth,* for the *material at issue,* over geology, paleontology, or psychology.

The time has come, even in a discursive epilogue, for return to the central topic, which is anxiety. Have these reflections on the context in which anxiety may be viewed—from physiological, psychiatric and psychological, and theological perspectives—provided a new way in which either to ask or to answer the question of what anxiety is? Has my underlying point carried conviction that whatever anxiety may be it is to be found somewhere within the total concrete process of perceiving, identifying, and dealing with danger and challenge—regardless of the nature, depth, ultimacy, or temporality of the danger or challenge?

Within the total concrete process by which a human being tries to meet danger or challenge, I suggest that anxiety is the capacity to send and receive a message concerning the presence of the danger or challenge. The message is both sent and received by the ego, although its content may come from a variety of sources. The basic structure out of which the capacity develops is given in precisely the sense that the capacity for language is given. But what the anxiety capacity will recognize or signal as danger is learned in experience by human beings, even though some parts of the content of danger will be universal.

The accuracy and relevance of the message that is sent is never independent of the history of the person. A color-blind man cannot send signals about red and green traffic lights. A person reared in a culture where one kind of action is approved will not send danger signals to himself about that simply because some other culture prohibits it. But even though the cultural and personal history conditions what is felt to be danger, and thus what the signals warn about, this is very far from saying that a person decides consciously what he wants to be warned of. The most dangerous dangers are those of which consciousness may be least aware. The capacity to signal, we might say, keeps up with development, as in the child who feels the warning signal if he tries to remain at one fixed stage and not move on. It is a message from himself to himself, but it contains a kind of lure element from the future as well as a thrust from the past.

There seems no good reason for selecting certain messages about catastrophic dangers and treating them as if they were categorically different from messages about small dangers, if it is the understanding of the process with which we are concerned. Nor should there be categorical separation about messages that warn of dangers we can handle by destroying and those we must handle by accepting. And if the message is accurate at the point of transmission and rings its alarm loudly, it should not be regarded as having failed if, on other grounds, the message cannot be heard, received, or heeded. In such a case not anxiety but something else has failed. Needed distinctions should be made in these as in other ways. But they are not categorical, and they are not about the process or function of anxiety as such.

This view holds that it is impossible to understand anxiety apart from its presence as a part of the larger concrete process of becoming aware of danger or challenge and taking whatever action is possible to meet or deal with it. Anxiety is not the total process of mobilization nor yet the failure of such mobilization. Anxiety is, first, the signal. The anxiety performs its function normatively if the danger is real and the signal is loud and clear. When the signal is heard and heeded, and the whole person is then able to take appropriately adaptive action, the signal is stilled until needed again. The experience of successful adaptation after hearing the signal sharpens the readiness to be alert next time. In this sense, even the anxiety increases its readiness as there is successful experience with heeding it.

I am here taking the position that anxiety is to be regarded, at least primarily, as a capacity to send and receive a signal about danger or challenge. In principle, this begins with Freud's later theory of anxiety, but regards this theory as capable of being generalized beyond what Freud attempted. It is my contention —until someone pokes holes in it—that anxiety in the fundamental sense means one thing and not two or more; and that all the necessary distinctions about types, forms, degrees, objects, and so on can be brought into a single world of discourse if we take seriously Freud's argument about anxiety as signal but generalize it beyond what he attempted.

This is a purposive, future-oriented, and even teleological conception of anxiety, in that it identifies anxiety (at least primarily) with a capacity which, if it were *not* present, would leave the person the helpless victim of every danger that appeared. This stress on *capacity* seems justified on virtually every reflective ground. Most striking of all is the psychiatric discovery that, even in the most extremely disorganized and distorted sufferers, the signaling system remains intact although the signals may be misinterpreted. But there are other cogent reasons as well. For instance, this view puts "fear" in its proper place, as the more or less immediate and correct interpretation of a clearly identified danger or challenge, whether the object is an approaching car that one may avoid or the intimation of mortality that one needs to confront. Once interpreted, defined, and confronted *in ways appropriate to the nature of the danger or challenge,* what anxiety has signaled about (both sending and receiving) becomes fear, and may be dealt with as such.

Another support to this view is its bringing "ontological anxiety" into the same universe of discourse as "neurotic anxiety" without denying a legitimate and important distinction between what these terms connote. If a man has long neglected serious reflection on his mortality, his guilt, his sin, or his finitude, the signal that warns him of his neglect is not *functionally* different from that which has caused him to accelerate his stride an hour earlier in evading an approaching jalopy. For his continuing existence, and his existence as a truly human being, the heeding of both signals is necessary. Why should it not be assumed that there is a unity in the signaling capacity of the organism (filtered through all kinds of conditionings in the perceptual apparatus, to be sure), whether the object of danger is cars or death? Eliminate one wholly from the organism, and it is inconceivable that the other could remain intact.

One can and indeed must say, as Tillich has said in one way and Pruyser in another, that "ontological anxiety" is more important for its attitudinal consequences than for its continuing affect, and that "neurotic anxiety" is more to be noted for its displacement of affect (perhaps through symptoms) than for its consciously accurate rendition of the danger. What my view asserts is that the warning function is being attempted in both instances, and that the intactness of the signaling apparatus should not necessarily be called in question because there are, or are not, adequate and appropriate interpretations of the message at headquarters and the mobilization of resources to meet the danger disclosed.

Such a view of anxiety brings Freud and Kierkegaard within a common world of discourse. For to Kierkegaard, hanging over the abyss, something he has not consciously contrived enables him to perceive that there *is* an abyss. To Freud it is some nonreducible capacity of the ego that enables the signal of danger (whether about approaching cars or unresolved Oedipus complexes) to be noted. As capacity for giving and receiving a signal, anxiety becomes a common denominator to both men.

Still another merit of this view is its clinical utility in relation to "jittery" affect. Every clinician has seen the so-called "anxious" patient, who streams perspiration, shakes with uncertainty, speaks with pitiful voice, and tells a heartrending story—but who, unlike the other sufferer who has just had a monumental signal and who shows all these signs while existentially contemplating whether or not to heed them, actually had the traumatic experience many years ago, and now simply repeats the physiological marks (or some of them) that appeared in the initial experience. To be sure, such persons do literally suffer, and they still require our sympathy. They are not malingerers. They have no notion that there is a "vain repetition" element in what they present to the world, that their current affect is partly bogus in contrast to the original situation that got them started. From the point of view of anxiety as signal, they are not "sufferers from anxiety" but instead are cultivators-of-anxiety-as-affect. Such an insight is both theoretically clarifying and therapeutically helpful.

Clinically also, this view should help us to recognize the intactness of the signaling systems of many persons who, because their interpretation of the signals is bizarre or maladaptive, are altogether too likely to be judged as "devoid of anxiety." The qualitative break may indeed have come, by which they have no conscious recognition of the true state of inner feelings, after which they substitute symptoms for concerned affect. But that does not necessarily mean that their signaling apparatus has broken down. And so long as this is intact, even their most fantastic or malign misinterpretations of its message cannot conceal the fact that a will to health, transcending conscious purpose, is still at work. The clinician who wants to acknowledge all the facts—of both impairment and resources—should be grateful to a theory that prevents him from saying the patient has no "anxiety" (as conscious affect), and which makes him conclude erroneously, therefore, that there is nothing within the patient working, as is he, toward therapeutic ends.

Since I cannot take this whole issue lightly, and have been delving into my more icebergian thoughts about it, I have a strong suspicion that I have been guilty latterly of an *ex cathedra* tone, running the risk of violating my earlier self-directed injunction not to take my own constructions on this subject too seriously. I have been arguing for the definition of anxiety as, primarily, the capacity to send and receive signals about danger or challenge, beginning with Freud's later theory and generalizing it beyond what he attempted. I have tried to show that such a procedure, when held within the overall context of the total human process of response to danger or challenge, clears up many problems at both the theoretical and clinical levels.

But I know that common sense is against me. And even though I have (I believe) Freud to keep me company, I still feel vulnerable. At my next case conference an intelligent psychiatrist is sure to call a jittery patient "anxious," and at the next one another competent physician is likely to say that a withdrawn or depressed patient is lacking in "anxiety." Despite Freud's theory, clinical practice has so firmly attached "anxiety" to a certain kind of consciously experienced affect that it would be folly to stop and argue the theoretical issue at every case conference. Yet common sense to the contrary, I believe the understanding of the dynamics of the patient and the appraisal of his resources can be improved by moving away from the naïve identification of "anxiety" with a certain order of conscious affect.

My view goes no less counter to the common sense of my theological brethren if, like Niebuhr and Tillich, they are appropriately concerned with anxiety and not, like Barth, disdainful of the whole idea in any form because it is about man rather than about God. The first thing done by my non-commonsense notion is, theologically speaking, to deny that anxiety is solely about man and not also about God. For if God is Creator and Redeemer, where else but in the signal to be alert to whatever danger or challenge one has hitherto neglected can be read the Voice of God? Where else can be found the work of grace that leads men to hear the Word of God? If my primary definition of anxiety is accepted, then it will be a great deal harder for theologians in the future to neglect it together on the grounds of its being pure "anthropology" than has been true in the past.

Unless I am gravely mistaken, my view does not go counter to what Kierkegaard and Niebuhr have said about the nature of anxiety, although both of them have toyed with anxiety as affect or feeling and not wholly dissociated themselves from this commonsense view. With Tillich the situation is quite different. He would easily and readily acknowledge anxiety as signal, but he would at once subvert my intention by calling it two or three other things at the same time. His thought has many merits, among them a strong conviction that the *acknowledgment* of anxiety as affect, or as condition of estrangement or of finitude, is itself constructive. He also suggests, quite correctly, that there is no categorical distinction among the forms of anxiety, however understood. Despite these great virtues, his theory is still impaired by remnants of the commonsense notion that if you don't feel it it isn't anxiety.

John Jones, age forty-five, may have a dream about wasting his powers, consult his minister the next day, begin serious reflections on the meaning of his life in the light of his mortality, his responsibility, and his sin, and be a more complete, happy, and productive human being as a result. Bill Smith, same age, may hear the same basic signal, interpret it as potential mental illness, go next day to consult his psychiatrist in a sweat, and talk existentially about possible suicide. These men are different; anyone, pastor or psychiatrist, who tries to help them must recognize the difference; and yet, at the level of hearing, heeding, and trying honestly to interpret a signal about something not obvious or obtrusive, both are identical. Both are, in the signal sense, "anxious." As an earlier generation put it, both are "anxious inquirers" about the way to salvation. Our forefathers may have been a bit light on the range and variety of the pathological responses to anxiety, but when the signal of anxiety was performing its proper function, their insight was quite in keeping with my suggestion.

My suggestion, practically speaking, is this, borrowing from what I have sometimes heard, colloquially, in psychoanalytic circles: Let us think of "anxiety" primarily as *signal;* and, for the time being, speak of "anxiety-signal" or "signal-anxiety." This is the primary phenomenon, the amazing and nonreducible capacity of even the most distorted human being still to receive signals about the real dangers and challenges, and applies equally to the capacity of the most "self-actualizing" person to send and receive signals about himself and his relation to the world.

But let me not wholly desert common sense. If one feels jittery, constricted, or woozy, someone will call it "anxiety," even if he has read this discussion; so let us arm for this in advance, and, without deterring him altogether, ask him to call it "affect-anxiety" or "anxiety-affect."

As to the hundreds of theological students I have met, all were convinced that they must *confront* "ontological anxiety," and a few of them were ready to admit they had best also *solve* "neurotic anxiety," the non-commonsense virtue of my definition is to make them all ask what is the danger or challenge, from past *or* future, they are being signaled to confront? Perhaps it exists, but I have never yet seen an "ontological anxiety" in pure concrete form. And yet, on the other hand, I have never seen a disturbed mental patient without some saving trace of "ontological anxiety."

An almost final word has to do with anxiety and creativity. If my definition is accepted, then the basic capacity of the human being to deal with, as danger or challenge, not only approaching lions and cars and mortality but also unresolved complexes and undiscovered meanings is no less a comment on the source of anxiety than it is on the source of creativity. But this point of view, at the same time, makes nonsense of the notion that anxiety (as affect) is the indispensable condition of creativity (as achievement). Kierkegaard rightly said that anxiety and creativity are two sides of the same coin. Both stem from the same uniquely human capacity which, when applied to dangers and challenges and acknowledged in concrete instances, we have called "anxiety."

Finally, how does the contribution of our several authors accord with the thesis I have been nascently developing? The exigencies of publishing being what they are, our authors may not have time to write their own epilogues. How does my thesis fit into what they have severally tried to say?

As to Ishak Ramzy's chapter, I am more deeply indebted to him than he realizes. His great contribution, much greater than his own claims for it, is in showing the development of Freud's thought about anxiety from early to later periods. My own constructive statement has begun from, and been deeply influenced by, Freud's final or mature theory of anxiety. Yet in my recapitulation of this theory and my attempt to set it within the total human process of dealing with danger or challenge, I have found myself dealing with the very factors of excitation, emotion, continuing tensions, and the like that were responsible for Freud's earlier theories. Had it not been for Ramzy's penetration, I should not have seen this relationship so clearly. All of this is, of course, very far from suggesting that Ramzy, or any of our other authors, agrees with my thesis statement.

Fred Berthold's thesis about anxious longing—that anxiety is the child of love even when love is frustrated, that anxiety includes desire as well as something negative—is certainly not negated by my position although this last may remind Berthold that he has not attempted to answer the question directly as I have posed it. Berthold reminds us further, wholly in line with my thesis, that the danger or challenge about which anxiety may warn us may include something missing—regardless of whether what is missing is something that may or should be got on its own terms, or instead is to be given up in favor of something else.

Charles A. Curran's presentation of the way in which "anxious striving" may persist through dark days and eventually bring light is thoroughly consistent with my thesis. Despite many temptations to the contrary, there is a healthy reluctance in "anxious striving" to take the easy path of cutting the connection between constrictive feeling and uninterpreted danger or challenge. Even though one is not sure of the nature of the danger, and even less sure of the way it may be met, the constrictive feeling (despite pain) may be retained, and experimental ways of dealing with it as well as interpreting its nature may be carried out. In this process there is normatively some painful affect, but it is not paralyzing. More ego strength is available than the person may realize. With these observations of Father Curran I am in enthusiastic agreement.

As to the remarkable and penetrating chapter by Albert C. Outler, who begins with Augustine and, as he might say, also ends with Augustine, there is happily some good, authentic Augustinian Outler somewhere in the middle. Augustine and Outler agree that, when the danger or challenge about which anxiety gives the signal lies in the realm of meaning and value, and adaptation may proceed only by confronting the larger or more ultimate questions of life and death, the empowerment needed for this confrontation can come only from God's grace.

161

As a Christian theologian, I agree most profoundly with this assertion. Beyond this, Outler implies, and maybe Augustine did too, that no instance of signaling about danger or challenge can be said to be devoid of grace, no matter how pathological the response to it may be nor however much it may be in conflict with "principalities and powers."

From Paul W. Pruyser and his penetrating chapter, I have learned so much that a comment seems like carrying coals to Newcastle. His own thesis, in my judgment, is in no necessary conflict with mine, even though he seems to pose "anxiety" as "affect" *or* as "cognitive state." In many ways, his thought is a better place at which to close off, temporarily, the discussion of this book than is my own thesis. For he has, in the manner of the true scholar, fully acknowledged the existing confusions and differences, and yet given both practical and theoretical clues to further study. I, on the other hand, impelled by my fantasies (and hopefully but not assuredly by some knowledge and imagination), have tried to present a unified definition of anxiety. Perhaps between us we may smoke out the truth: he by finding people who agree with his division for the right or the wrong reasons, and I by evoking those who agree with my unified view for the right or the wrong reasons.

It is altogether likely that the years ahead will see new light shed on the nature and meaning of anxiety by all the human sciences: physiology, psychology, sociology, cultural anthropology, and others. But as Freud saw clearly, something in addition to new data is needed. This epilogue has argued that the nature of that something added is contextual in nature. Whether or not that proves a valuable clue, it is certain that an increase in our understanding of anxiety must involve both scientific study and theoretical reflection. In this task, psychiatry has a manifestly important place. But theology can also consider new data and think new thoughts, and it may well do so about anxiety.

Contributors Biographical Notes

FRED BERTHOLD, JR., is professor of religion at Dartmouth College. He holds the Ph.D. degree from the University of Chicago. He is author of *The Fear of God* (1959) and is co-editor of *Basic Sources of the Judaeo-Christian Tradition* (1962).

CHARLES A. CURRAN is professor of psychology at Loyola University, Chicago. A Roman Catholic priest, he received the Ph.D. degree from Ohio State University. He has published *Personality Factors in Counseling* (1947), *Counseling in Catholic Life and Education* (1952), and many articles. He is a consultant to The Menninger Foundation.

SEWARD HILTNER is professor of theology and personality at Princeton Theological Seminary. A Presbyterian minister, he received the Ph.D. degree from the University of Chicago. He has published several books including *Preface to Pastoral Theology* (1958). He is a consultant to The Menninger Foundation.

KARL MENNINGER is chief of staff of The Menninger Foundation. He received the M.D. degree from the Harvard Medical School. The two most recent of his many books are a completely revised edition of his *Manual for Psychiatric Case Study* (1963) and *The Vital Balance* (1963), a theoretical textbook of psychiatry. Some of his many articles have been published as *A Psychiatrist's World* (1960) and in the *Bulletin of the Menninger Clinic*.

ALBERT C. OUTLER is professor of theology at Perkins School of Theology, Southern Methodist University. He received the Ph.D. degree from Yale University. He is author of several books including *Pychotherapy and the Christian Message* (1953); he edited and translated *The Confessions and Enchiridion of St. Augustine* (1955), and has contributed many articles to various theological journals.

PAUL W. PRUYSER is director of the department of education of The Menninger Foundation. He received the Ph.D. degree from Boston University after early education in Holland. He is co-author with Karl Menninger of several books and articles. He is consultant to the Board of Christian Education of the United Presbyterian Church and visiting lecturer in clinical psychology at McCormick Theological Seminary.

CONSTRUCTIVE ASPECTS OF ANXIETY

ISHAK RAMZY is a training analyst in the Topeka Institute for Psychoanalysis and a staff member of The Menninger Foundation. He received his M.A. degree from the University of Cairo (Egypt) and his Ph.D. degree from the University of London (England). He is author of several books (in Arabic) and many articles (in English and French) in psychology and psychoanalysis. Among his recent contributions are "From Aristotle to Freud" (*Bulletin of The Menninger Clinic*, Vol. XX) and "The Range and Spirit of Psychoanalytic Technique" (*The International Journal of Psycho-Analysis*, Vol. XLII).

Index

The editors acknowledge with appreciation the work of Mrs. Mary Douglas Lee in constructing the index.

Abashment, 17
Abraham, 130
Abstinence, 20
Abyss, 54, 75, 94, 97, 152, 156
Acceptance, 85, 108, 111
Adamic myth, 75, 78, 79, 82
Adaptation, 127, 161
  affect and, 38, 44
  capacity for, 40
  danger and, 39, 146-49
  hysteria and, 42
  symptoms vs., 37-40
Adjustment; *see also* Adaptation
Adolescence, 20, 94
Aesthetic anxiety, 57
Affect
  alarm and, 49
  anxiety and, 37, 44, 48, 60, 65, 89-90, 99, 121, 129, 134, 138-39, 145, 158-62
  cultivators of anxiety, 157
  danger and, 42
  displacement of, 156
  instincts and, 132
  lack of, 157
  levels of, 39
  pain of, 64
  paralyzing, 39, 61
  psychiatric treatment and, 44
  psychic dread as, 92
  teleological, 132
  withdrawal and, 58
Aggression, 22, 58, 70
Agoraphobia, 20
Alarm
  affect and, 49
  signal, 35, 72, 89

syndrome, 90
Alertness, 45, 64, 152, 158
  anxiety as, 90, 145
  capacity for, 47
  to danger, 39, 146
Ali ibn Hazm, 122
Alienation, 93, 150
Altschule, M. D., 125
Anguish, 17
Anger, 70
Angst, 25, 38, 89
Animal nature, 25
Animals, 72, 126
Anthropologists, 49
Anxiety
  acute, 127
  affect as, 37, 44, 48, 60, 65, 89-90, 99, 121, 129, 134, 138-39, 145, 158-62
  alarm signal as, 35-37, 45, 72, 89, 145, 153-55, 158-61
  alertness as, 90, 145
  in animals, 126
  apprehension as, 17, 40-41, 43, 49, 90, 121
  capacity for, 155, 157
  categories of 45, 57
  cognitive state as, 58, 61, 63, 65, 121-41, 162
  confrontation of, 64-65, 145, 151-52, 161
  constructive, 35, 58, 92
  consummation and, 81
  creativity and, 26, 57, 59-60, 63, 69-71, 74-75, 77-78, 81-84, 92, 99, 122, 133, 160
  danger in, 23, 82, 89, 145
  defined, 17, 24, 38, 48, 63, 72, 89, 93, 95, 99, 121-22, 155, 162

destructive, 58, 90, 96, 100, 134, 140
disteleological, 69
etiology of, 20
existential, 62, 64-65, 90, 129, 135-39
fear vs., 47, 71, 81
failure of, 58
forced, 132
freedom and, 55, 131
Freud on, 17, 155, 160
function of, 35, 48, 58
grace and, 89, 99, 101
guilt and, 81, 133
human nature and, 69
identified, 155
Kierkegaard on, 53-59
lack of, 157
longing as, 69, 72, 96, 101, 105, 114, 116, 129, 161
love and, 24, 71, 79, 83, 90, 101, 129
May on, 49
molecular concepts of, 122
moral, 45, 57, 91
morbid, 81, 126
negation and, 37, 62, 90
neurosis and, 20, 45, 62, 69, 75, 91, 100, 125, 155-56, 160
Niebuhr on, 59-61
objective, 25, 45
pain and, 34
paralyzing, 49
pathological, 45, 57, 62, 64-65
positive, 105, 112, 114, 140
preparedness, 46-47
primal, 96
psychiatric theories of, 33
psychological reactions to, 127
quantity of, 70
reduction of, 100, 127
relief of, 25
religious theories of, 53-59, 73
reversible, 71
sin and, 54, 59, 77, 79, 82, 130-31, 133, 150-51, 155
source of, 115
striving and, 105-6, 116, 161
structure of, 75
subjectively experienced, 121
theory of, 33, 53-69, 73
Tillich on, 61-65
true, 45
vulnerabilities in, 49
Appetites, 96

Appetition, 90, 96
Apprehension, 17, 40-41, 43, 49, 90, 121
Aristotle, 16
Arrogance, 95
Art, 26, 121
Artificiality, 110
Atheists, 150
Atomic theory, 16
Augustine, 53, 85, 87-102, 116, 129, 161
Autonomic nervous system, 127
Aversion, 97
Avicenna, 19
Avoidance mechanisms, 37, 43, 57
Awareness, 90, 92, 133, 152; see also Alertness

Barth, Karl, 99
Behavior, 38, 123, 126
Being, 61, 93, 135
Bereavement, 150
Berthold, Fred, 161
Biology, 19
Birth, 34, 46, 108, 131, 138
Blindness, 126
Body, 19
Boss, 151
Bottomless pit, 94
Brain, 18, 49, 126
Breathing, 38; see also Constriction
Brown-Sequard, C. E., 125
Brücke, Ernst, 16
Bunyan, John, 80

Castration, 46, 72
Catatonia, 77, 82
Catholicism, 105
Challenge, 145, 147-48, 152-54, 157-58, 161
Chesterton, G. K., 106
Choice, 56, 60, 97, 135, 138
Christianity, 56, 130, 144, 151
  anxiety and, 105, 131
  theologians of, 92, 94, 150
Climacteric, 20
Cognition, 92, 134, 137
  anxiety as, 90-91
  effects of, 100
  emotion vs., 123
  state of, 58, 61, 63, 65, 121-41, 162
Color blindness, 153
Commitment, 117

Communication, 92, 113
Communion, 93, 113
Compulsion neurosis, 38, 77
Concept of Dread, 54
Concern, 150
Condemnation, 62
Confessions, 93
Conflict, 25, 27, 112
Confrontation, 64-65, 145, 148, 151-52, 161
Confusion, 17
Conscience, 20
Consciousness
    affect and, 40
    levels of, 126
Consensual validation, 122
Constriction, 38-39, 41, 44-45, 159, 161
Consummation, 81
Continuity, 19
Contrition, 17
Control, 25
Contuition, 98
Conversion, 94
Conversion hysteria, 42, 125
Convulsions, 126
Coping devices, 46, 57, 78, 110, 127
CORINTHIANS
    I:13:11, 107
    I:15:55, 117
    I:15:58, 101
Counseling, 103, 106-7, 111-13, 116
Courage, 97, 101, 151
Creativity, 26, 57, 59-60, 63, 69-71, 74-75, 77-78, 81-84, 92, 99, 122, 133, 160
Cure, 101
Curran, Charles, 161

Damnation, 98-99
Danger, 81, 152-54, 157-58, 161
    adaptation to, 39, 146-49
    affect and, 42
    anxiety and, 23, 82, 89, 145
    confrontation of, 148, 151-52
    fear of, 25
    frustrated excitation and, 48
    identified, 47
    mental health and, 149
    messages of, 154
    perception and, 44, 148
    psychology and, 149
    reaction to, 38

    real, 146-47, 152
    sensitivity to, 90
    signal of, 35, 72, 89
    symptoms to avoid, 35, 44
    theology and, 149
Darwin, Charles, 15, 124
Death, 76, 117, 134, 138-39, 150, 155
    anxiety of, 62, 64, 82, 97
    Augustine and, 97
    threat of, 65
    wishes, 22
Deception, 111
Defense, 46, 57, 78, 110, 127
    anxiety and, 80
    avoidance, 37, 43, 57
    danger and, 149
    reaction of, 126
    symptoms and, 36
Defiance, 152
Degradation, 91
Denial, 37, 62, 90
Dependency, 107, 133-34, 152
Depression, 17, 130
Deprivation, 90, 99
Desires, 80-81, 90
Despair, 28, 64, 123, 130
Destiny, 130
Destructive urges, 22, 58, 70
Determinism, 97
Devil, 138
Diagnosis, 112
Discontent, 77
Disequilibrium, 93-94
Displacement, 156
Disteleological anxiety, 81
Dizziness, 55-56, 131
Doctor, 95, 98
Dr. Faustus, 75
Dread, 17, 40, 90, 95, 99, 129, 138; *see also* Anxiety
Dreams, 22, 54
Drives, 71
Drugs, 22
Dual instinct theory, 58, 70
Dynamics, 99, 116

Edwards, Jonathan, 131
Ego
    anxiety and, 23, 45, 48, 156
    conflicts and, 112
    confrontation and, 65
    danger and, 48

failure of, 37
functions of, 23
ideal, 25
psychology, 128
regulatory devices of, 46, 57, 78, 110, 127
restriction of, 77
strength of, 43, 65, 161
Einstein, Albert, 15
Electrotherapy, 22
Embarrassment, 17
Emotions; *see also* Affect
anxiety and, 90, 128, 135
cognition vs., 123
control of, 146
danger and, 145-46, 148
physiology of, 145
psyche-soma and, 126
psychology and, 121, 147
self and, 39
Empathy, 121, 130
Emptiness, 62, 65
Encyclopaedia Britannica, 125
Energy, 146
Environment, 91
Epilepsy, 124, 126
Equilibrium, 93-95, 131
Erotism, 21
Escape, 27
Estrangement, 97
Ethics, 27
Evil, 131
Excitation, 147
Existential anxiety, 62, 64-65, 90, 129, 135-39
Existentialism, 53, 69, 91, 134, 150-51
EXODUS
20:18-21, 73
Expectation, 98

Faith, 28, 114, 134
dread and, 100
self-commitment and, 113
Family relations, 28
Fantasy, 27, 100
Fear, 25, 84, 117, 121-24, 130, 135-37, 155
Adamic myth and, 79
animals and, 126
anxiety vs., 47, 71, 81
of falling, 93
of God, 74, 107

of horses, 72
infants and, 24
of loss, 23, 79, 90-91, 99, 101, 138
love and, 83, 101
morbid, 81, 126
objective, 25, 62
physiology and, 147
rational, 42
sin and, 73
teleological, 69
of unknown, 78
self, 39
Fight, 145
Finiteness, 133, 135, 137, 150-51, 155
Flight, 145
Foreverness, 44
Forgiveness, 85
Freedom, 54, 57, 65, 76, 96, 129-30, 133-34
anxiety and, 55, 131
causality and, 98
confrontation and, 65
God and, 97
to grow, 114
Heidegger on, 132
Kierkegaard on, 55
radical, 75
reality and, 97
sin and, 55, 59
treatment and, 60, 69
Freud, Sigmund, 15-21, 24, 33-34, 37-38, 40, 42-49, 53, 57-58, 64-65, 67, 69-74, 77, 79, 81, 89-91, 112, 115-16, 122, 125-26, 129, 132, 136, 138, 143-44, 155-58, 160, 162
Fright, 123
Frustrated excitation, 48
Frustration, 90
Fulfillment, 105

Galen, 19
Gallahue Conference, 33, 143
Gastrointestinal disorders, 20
GENESIS
1:5-6, 76
1:28, 75
Geology, 153
German language, 25, 38, 89
Gilson, Etienne, 103, 115
God, 82-84, 92-93, 95, 107, 109, 113-17, 132, 138, 152, 158
Godlikeness, 76

Goethe, 15, 16
Goldstein, Kurt, 49
Good, 131
Grace, 96, 98, 102, 133, 151, 158, 161
    anxiety and, 89, 99, 101
    defined, 97
    the elect and, 98
    irresistible, 98
    love as, 85, 101
Gratification, 24
Gratitude, 98, 152
Griesinger, Wilhelm, 124
Groundlessness, 93-95, 97, 99, 101
Growth, 111, 122
Guilt, 17, 62, 77, 79, 84, 128, 133, 150-
    51, 155
    Adamic myth and, 79
    anxiety and, 81, 133
    separation and, 79
Guislain, J., 124

Hall, G. Stanley, 107
Hans, 41, 72-73, 81
Happiness, 95-96
Hate, 58, 70
Haughtiness, 95
Healing, 63, 80, 117
Health, 96
Hebrew language, 73
Hebrew theology, 150
Heidegger, Martin, 69-70, 91, 132-33,
    136, 139
Helplessness, 24-25
Heraclitus, 135
Hippo, 95
Honesty, 112
Hope, 112, 114
Horror, 138
Horses, 72
Hospital, mental, 129
Hostility; see also Aggression
Human condition, 92
Human nature, 69
Hunger, 151
Hurt, 40
Hypnosis, 22
Hysteria, 42, 125

Id, 46, 95, 112
Idolatry, 93
Ignorance, 76, 84

Inadequacy, 116
Infancy, 24
Infantile guilt, 28
Infantile sexuality, 22
Inhibitions, 23, 134
Inhibitions, Symptoms and Anxiety, 23
Innocence, 54, 56, 84, 131
Insanity, 124
Insecurity, 94
Insight, 91, 97
Instincts, 25, 58, 70, 101, 108, 132, 134
Intellect, 99
Interpersonal relations, 49, 92
Interpretation of Dreams, 22
Interview, 100, 108
Isaac, 130

James, William, 131
Janet, P., 125-26
Jackson, John Hughlings, 124, 126
Jesus, 29
Jewish language, 73
Jewish theologians, 105, 150
Jitteriness, 156, 159
JOB
    3:25, 8
JOHN
    4:10, 114
    4:16, 115
    4:20, 115
    20:25, 17
Jones, Ernest, 21
Jones, John, 159
Judaism, 105
Jung, C. G., 149

Kaufmann, Walter, 136
Kierkegaard, Sören, 33, 51, 53-58, 60,
    64-65, 70, 75, 78, 119, 129-33, 138,
    144, 156, 158, 160
Knowledge, 71
Kraepelin, Emil, 126

Language
    capacity, 153
    German, 25, 38, 89
    Hebrew, 73
Learning, 39, 71, 127
Leavy, Stanley, 89
Libido, 97, 122
Liddell, Howard, 49
Life, 15

Logic, 16, 99
London, 106
Loneliness, 25
Longing, 69, 72, 96, 101, 105, 114, 116, 129, 161
Loss, 23, 69, 90-91, 99, 101, 138
Love, 101, 108, 134
  anxiety and, 24, 71, 79, 83, 90, 101, 129
  blocked, 84
  course of, 84
  divine, 83, 95-96, 107-8, 111, 113-15, 117
  grace as, 85, 98
  hate vs., 70
  longing and, 96
  loss of, 46, 101
  mature, 84
  narcissistic, 79
  nature, and, 15
  object, 79, 81
  psychiatric treatment and, 99
  religion and, 112-13
  union and, 80
Löwenfeld, Leopold, 21
LUKE
  6:41, 26
Luther, Martin, 83, 130, 137

Magical thinking, 91, 93, 100
Malingerers, 156
Manichees, 94
Massage, 22
Mastery, 38, 78
Maturity, 84, 105-7, 112
May, Rollo, 33, 49
Meaninglessness, 62, 65, 94
Medicine, 21
Mediterranean, 18
Memory, 98
Menninger Foundation, 143
Menninger, Karl, 43, 143
Mental health, 149
Mental hospital, 129
Mental illness, 124-25, 159
  catatonia as, 77, 82
  depression as, 17, 130
  neurasthenia as, 20, 125
  treatment of, 18
  unitary concept of, 43
Metaphysics, 92
Meynert, Theodor, 125

Mind, 19
Mobilization, 146
Mohammed, 29
Moral anxiety, 45, 57, 91
Morality, 22
Morbid anxiety, 81, 126
Mortality, 151, 155
Moses, 29
Mother-infant relations, 24
Motivation, 27, 127
  creativity as, 26
  knowledge of, 71
Motor tension, 46
Mourning, 150
Music, 26
Mysticism, 80

Narcissism, 79
Nature, 15, 56, 126
Negation, 37, 62, 90
Nervous system, 18, 49, 126-27
Neurasthenia, 20, 125
Neurology, 19
Neuropsychiatry, 18; see also Psychiatry
Neurosis, 21, 28, 42
  animal, 126
  compulsion, 38, 77
  religion and, 28
  repetition in, 38
Neurotic anxiety, 20, 45, 62, 69, 75, 91, 100, 125, 155-56, 160
Neutralization, 147
New Yorker, The, 153
Niebuhr, Reinhold, 33, 51, 53, 59-61, 64-65, 133, 158
Nonbeing, 62, 135
Nothingness, 138

Obedience, 130
Object love, 79, 81
Objective anxiety, 25, 45
Obsession, 28
Ocean, 94
Odier, Charles, 91
Oedipus complex, 35, 150-51, 156
Ontogeny, 107
Ontological anxiety, 61, 90, 95-96, 100-1, 155-56, 159
Ontology, 139
Original sin, 79, 131
Outler, Albert C., 53, 161

Pain, 19, 34, 45, 64, 131, 138
  constructive aspects of, 91
  insensitivity to, 126
  physical, 44
  psychic, 39
  retreat from, 57
Paintings, 114
Paleontology, 153
Panic, 17, 42, 123, 126
Paradise, 83
Pascal, G. R., 99
Pastor, 130
Pathological anxiety, 45, 57, 62, 64-65
Pathology, 45, 55, 57, 62, 64-65
Paul (Saul of Tarsus), 101, 107, 115, 117
Peace, 95
Peace of mind, 18
Pelagians, 98
Perception, 23-24,
  of danger, 44, 148
  undischarged tension and, 147
Perfection, 25, 56
Personality
  anxiety and, 129
  conflicts in, 63
  dual instincts in, 58, 70
  ego controls in, 46
  multiple, 126
Phallic symbols, 47, 89
Philistines, 150
Philosophy, 61
Phobias, 20, 41-42, 73, 126
Phylogeny, 107
Physician, 95, 98
Physiology, 16, 18, 20, 145
Pie, 152
Pity, 41
Pleasure, 19
Plotinian ecstasy, 94
Plotinian idealism, 97
Positive anxiety, 105, 112, 114, 140
Possession, 115
Possibility, 55, 76
Prayer, 111, 113
Predestination, 98-99
Prediction, 98
Preparedness, 46-47
Preservation, 81
Pride, 26, 59-60, 95, 133
Primal anxiety, 96
Problem-solving, 136

Protection, 24, 90
PROVERBS
  4:23, 92
Pruyser, Paul, 58, 61, 63, 65, 143, 156, 162
PSALMS
  2:11-12, 74
  5:7, 74
  25:14, 67, 74
  88:16, 8
  94:22, 115
Psyche-soma, 126
Psychic pain, 39
Psychic dread, 92
Psychiatry, 35, 84, 92, 100, 129
  anxiety and, 33-53, 143, 162
  interview, 100
  treatment 18, 42, 44, 60, 99
Psychoanalysis, 49, 85, 124
  anxiety theory in, 34-35, 71
  Freud and, 21
Psychoanalyst, 25
Psychoanalytic psychology, 27
Psychogenesis, 21
Psychological functioning, 19, 23-24
Psychology, 22, 153
  challenge and, 149
  danger and, 149
  depth, 70
  dying and, 139
  experimental, 127
  ontology and, 139
Psychosomatic medicine, 112, 116
Psychotherapy, 49, 112, 116; see also
    Psychiatry, Psychoanalysis
  causality and, 98
  maturity and, 106
Punishment,
  Adamic myth and, 79
  secondary gain as, 37
  separation as, 79

Rage, 25, 147
Ramzy, Ishak, 33-34, 47-48, 160
Rank, Otto, 46, 132
Reason, 28
Recollection, 98
Redemption, 114
Reformation, 62, 82, 84
Regulatory devices, 46, 57, 78, 110, 127
Rejection, 90, 108

Religion, 28, 56-57, 71, 73, 77, 79, 98, 100, 105, 111, 131
  anxiety, theories in, 53-69, 73
  counseling and, 112
  maturity and, 107
  oriental, 116
  theologians and, 92, 94, 150
  treatment and, 96, 112, 116
  values and, 107
Religiosity, 93, 100
Remorse, 17
Repetition
  compulsion, 38
  trauma and, 156
Repression, 36, 40, 48 ,
Respect, 111
Responsibility, 59, 105, 112
Restlessness, 101, 116
Reversible anxiety, 71
Roman Catholicism, 82
Rush, Benjamin, 124, 126, 128

Salvation, 159
Sartre, Jean Paul, 150-51
Science, 16, 26
Secondary gain, 36-37
Security, 78, 105
Self-awareness, 92
Self-control, 25
Self-pity, 41
Self-preservation, 81
Self-respect, 111
Self-sufficiency, 78-79
Self-transcendence, 47, 59-60
Self-understanding, 91, 97, 111
Selye, Hans, 112
Sensory attention, 46
Sensuality, 59
Separation, 23, 72, 79, 81, 83, 138
  anxiety and, 23, 79
  guilt and, 79
  from Mother, 24
  sin and, 74, 78
Serenity, 101
Sexuality
  anxiety and, 20
  infantile, 22
  perversion in, 71
Siblings, 151
Sickness, 130
Signal
  alarm syndrome as, 90

anxiety, 35-37, 45, 49, 72, 89, 145, 153-55, 158-61
  capacity to, 37
  danger, 35
  suicide as, 159
Sin, 59, 77, 79, 82, 130-31, 150-51, 155
  anxiety and, 54, 59, 133
  capacity for, 60
  choice and, 56
  creativity and, 59
  defined, 54, 59
  fear and, 73
  freedom and, 55
  original, 54, 131, 133
  separation and, 74
  sickness and, 130
Sky, 152
Smith, Bill, 159
Snakes, 47
Sorrow, 150
Spencer, Herbert, 124
Spirit, 56
Stekel, Wilhelm, 21
Stoicism, 150-51
Stress, 25, 27, 112, 123; *see also* Anxiety, Tension
Striving, 105-6, 116, 161
Subjective anxiety, 121
Sublimation, 27, 96
Suffering, 41, 85, 156
Suicide, 159
Sullivan, H. S., 49
Superego
  Augustine and, 95
  conflicts of, 112
  moral anxiety and, 46
  religion and, 77
Supernatural, 112
Superstition, 93
Symbols, 47, 89, 93
Sympathy, 156
Symptoms
  vs. adaptation, 37-40
  anxiety and, 42-43, 89, 91, 94, 99, 156
  danger and, 35
  as defense, 36
  as ego failure, 37
  inhibition and, 23
  loved object and, 80
Szasz, Thomas, 122

Talent, 27
Teaching, 70
Teleology, 69, 81, 132
Temperament, 148
Temptation, 56, 59, 61, 78, 84, 130, 151-52
Ten Commandments, 73
Tennant, Stephen, 114
Tension
  awareness of, 123
  frustration and, 24
  motor, 46
  psychic, 99
  undischarged, 147
Teresa of Avila, 80
Terror, 17, 123
Theology, 84, 151
  anxiety and, 16, 53-69, 82, 91, 129-30, 143
  danger and, 149
  psychiatry and, 100
  psychoanalysis and, 152
Time, 98
Therapy; see also Treatment
Thomas, Dylan, 96
Threat, 72
Tillich, Paul, 33, 51, 53, 61-65, 90, 135-37, 150, 156, 158
Timidity, 17
Titchener, E. B., 136
Tranquility, 100
Transcendence, 47, 59-60
Transiency, 105
Trauma, 34, 46, 131, 138
Treatment; see also, Psychiatry, Psychoanalysis, Psychotherapy
  accessibility to, 44
  anxiety and, 63, 123, 157
  freedom and, 60
  Freud and, 22
  psychiatric, 18, 42, 44, 60, 99

  psychoanalysis and, 25
  religion and, 96, 112, 116
  trust and, 113
True anxiety, 45
Trust, 113
Truth, 111
Tuke, Daniel, 125

Uncertainty, 94
Uneasiness, 60, 90, 101
Unconscious, 22, 40; see also Id
Understanding, 85, 91, 97, 111
Union, 80
Unitary concept, 43
Unworthiness, 84-85

Vandals, 95
Values, 135, 161
  maturity and, 106
  religious, 116
  secular, 107
  spiritual, 110
  system of, 128
  ultimate, 115
Vanity, 26
Vigilance, 49
Virginal anxiety, 20
Vulnerability, 49

Warning; see also Alarm
Watson, J. B., 122
Widows, 20
Will, 95, 136
Windelband, Wilhelm, 92
Withdrawal, 58
Wooziness, 159
Worthiness, 85, 108
Worthlessness, 108, 110
Writing, 26, 121
Wuerzburg School, 136